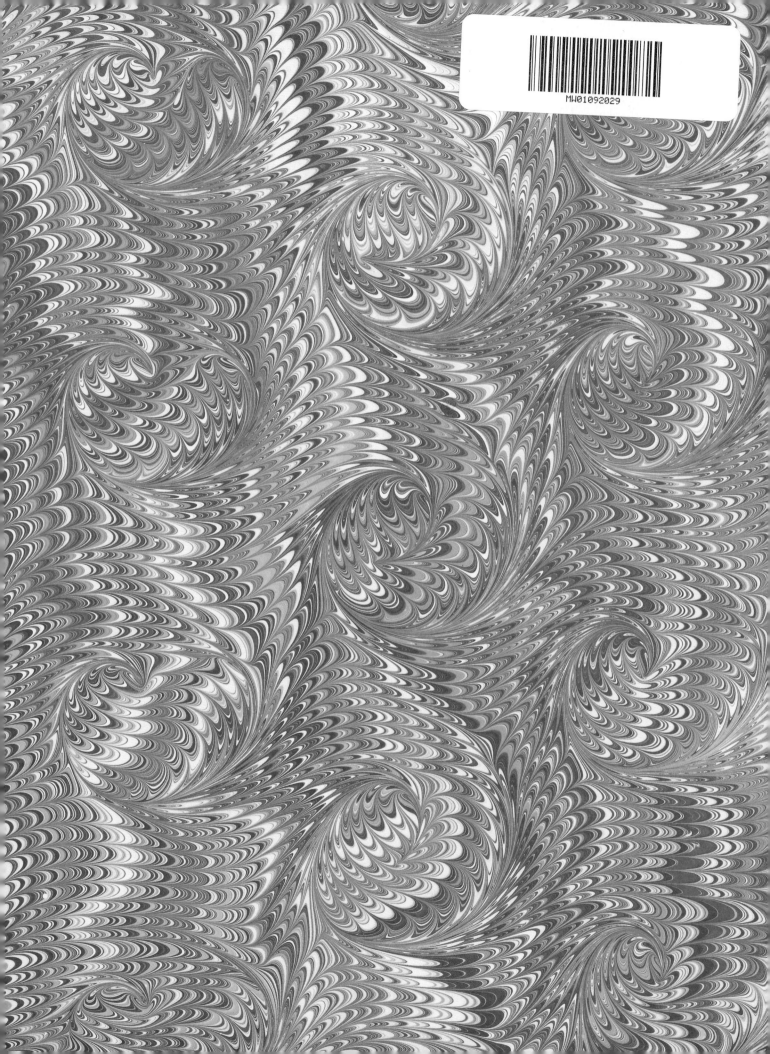

The 363rd Fighter Group in World War II

Also by the Author

FIGHTER UNITS & PILOTS OF THE 8TH AIR FORCE: SEPTEMBER 1942 - MAY 1945

Volume 1: Day-to-Day Operations • Fighter Group Histories

Volume 2: Aerial Victories • Ace Data

THE 363RD FIGHTER GROUP
in World War II
in Action over Europe with the P-51 Mustang

Kent D. Miller

Schiffer Military History
Atglen, PA

Dust jacket and aircraft profile artwork by S.W. Ferguson, Colorado Springs, CO.

On the dust jacket
On April 13, 1944, the 363rd Fighter Group flew a withdrawal support mission from the Halle area. Several enemy fighters were seen on the mission and two were shot down. One was an Me 109 which fell northeast of Stuttgart to Lt. Robert B. McGee of the 382nd Fighter Squadron flying his P-51B "Virginia". McGee would later add three more kills to become the highest scoring (aerial victories only) pilot in the group.

Book design by Robert Biondi.

Copyright © 2002 by Kent D. Miller.
Library of Congress Catalog Number: 2002102719.

Printed in China.
ISBN: 0-7643-1629-X

We are always looking for people to write books on new and related subjects. If you have an idea for a book, please contact us at the address below.

Published by Schiffer Publishing Ltd.
4880 Lower Valley Road
Atglen, PA 19310
Phone: (610) 593-1777
FAX: (610) 593-2002
E-mail: Schifferbk@aol.com.
Visit our web site at: www.schifferbooks.com
Please write for a free catalog.
This book may be purchased from the publisher.
Please include $3.95 postage.
Try your bookstore first.

In Europe, Schiffer books are distributed by:
Bushwood Books
6 Marksbury Ave.
Kew Gardens
Surrey TW9 4JF
England
Phone: 44 (0)208 392-8585
FAX: 44 (0)208 392-9876
E-mail: Bushwd@aol.com.
Free postage in the UK. Europe: air mail at cost.
Try your bookstore first.

Contents

Introduction

This is the story of a 9th Air Force fighter group which was active in Europe during World War II. The 363rd flew in combat for seven months until the rapid advance of Allied ground troops necessitated the group becoming a Tactical Recon unit.

The 363rd Fighter Group was the third Army Air Force unit in England to be equipped with the P-51 "Mustang", and early missions saw the pilots used as escort for the heavy bombers of the 8th Air Force. With the invasion of France in June of 1944, the 363rd's activities turned to a more tactical nature, in keeping with the overall 9th Air Force mission in Europe. This change also meant the group was used in a more defensive role-covering the ground forces' advance, protecting supply lines, shipping ports, etc. As such, their chances of meeting enemy aircraft, especially in July and August of 1944, were slim.

Due to their low victory to loss ratio (approximately 1:1) the 363rd has earned a negative reputation. But, when looking at the mission given to the group, especially from June onwards, this criticism is without merit. One has to keep in mind, as well, that losses included in this ratio are from all causes, not just plane-versus-plane combat.

To help explain the situation, consider these words from James Tipton, former commander of the 363rd:

"The invasion vehicles and beachhead must be preserved from crippling air attacks at all costs. This called for air defense, pure and simple, the country cousin of air offense but an essential element of the air superiority battle none the less. The 354th Group became the hunter, ranging far in advance and seeking the enemy before he could attack. We became the watchdog, the reserve in the rear to fend against wolves who might slip through the forward screen. For the most part, our role consisted of monotonous patrols over the crowded sea routes crossing the Channel and over the beachheads. Later, when XIX TAC moved to Normandy, the 363rd was established at an airfield closest to the Channel from whence we continued air defense, surveillance of our forces on the Continent, and the shipping which supplied them with men and munitions. The relative experience and records of the two P-51 groups made any other arrangement illogical."

It is hoped that the story presented in the following pages will shed some light on the true activities and achievements of the 363rd. The history could not be told without the help of the men who served with the group, and at this time I would like to thank those who supplied information and photographs: Fred Munder, James Brink, David Wolf, Lee Webster, Edward Vesely, Gordon McEachron, James Hill, Richard Lucas, Paul Maxwell, Joe Thoresz, Charles Smith, Joe Santarlasci, William Bullard, Lloyd Bruce, John Robertson, John Brown, George Peterson, Curry Wilson, Elmer Odell. Felix Kozaczka, Walter McKinney, Charles Reddig, Charles Stuart, Norman Ott, Morton Kammerlohr, Don Boatright, Gerald Clough, George J. Brooks, James Clark, Richard Asbury, Morris Easterly, Robert MacDonald, William Turner, Stan Gardner, Mike Scirocco, Hugo Pressnall, Evan McCall, Wallace King, Edward Kemmerer, Charles Moyle, James Christensen, Herbert Valentine, Howard Mosier, George Henning, Bruce Turner, Neill Ullo, Wallace Goodhue, Charles Shiff, Cyrus Christensen, Bernard Quinn, Robert Proctor, and Peter Bedrosian.

Also, thanks go to Ted Damick, Tom Ivie, William Hess, Talmadge Ambrose, Richard Ray, Gene Lamar, Richard Ray, Joyce Watson, Barbie Rench, James Crow, and the staffs of the Air Force Museum and Air Force Historical Research Center at Maxwell, Alabama.

Finally, a special acknowledgment to Steve Blake, who originally conceived the idea of a full 363rd history. Steve did a wonderful series of articles a number of years ago on the group which provided the basis for contacts, photos, and other information used in the preparation of this history. He was always more than willing to assist in any way possible, and for his interest and help I am deeply appreciative.

Kent D. Miller
Hicksville, Ohio
September 2001

The 363rd Fighter Group in World War II

Following is the history of the 363rd Fighter Group. All 411 missions are covered, with details including (where known), the leader, times up and down, details of the flight, claims made, and losses. Scoring is recorded in this manner: 0-0-0 is destroyed-probable-damaged (in the air) and 0-0 is destroyed-damaged (on ground claims). Interspersed among the missions are other activities of the 363rd and quotes from the group and squadron diaries. Following the text are extensive appendices adding more detail to the unit's history.

The 363rd Fighter Group flew an assortment of missions during its short combat tenure. The reader may find it helpful to understand what each mission involved so brief descriptions follow:

Bomber Escort
As with most of the early 9th Air Force units arriving in England, the 363rd found itself involved primarily with escorting 8th Air Force bombers over the Continent. Early missions were withdrawal supports, escorting the bombers back out over enemy territory after they had hit their targets. Other types of escort included penetration and target support, taking the bombers in and watching over them during their runs into and over the target area. Except for three missions in late June of 1944, the 363rd was done with 8th Air Force escorts by the end of May. June and July saw a few C-47 (troop carriers) escorts as well as 9th Air Force medium bomber escorts. These were normally flown, though not always, by less than group-strength formations. July and August also saw a number of fighter-bomber escorts for 9th Air Force planes attacking ground targets.

Sweep
This was either a group or squadron-strength mission designed to cover or "sweep" an assigned area. Usually targets of opportunity were strafed if no enemy aircraft or airfields presented themselves. Bombs were sometimes carried but few sweeps were thus flown.

Area Patrol
These were similar to a sweep though they were usually carried out in conjunction with escorting bombers or fighter-bombers. While the bombers or other aircraft attacked targets, the P-51s would patrol, keeping an eye out for enemy planes or other activity which might threaten Allied pilots in the area.

Dive Bombing
This was simply attacking ground targets with bombs. Normal procedure was for the majority of planes on a mission to carry out the bombing with one or more flights assigned as top cover. These missions began in March and grew rapidly through June. During July and August few dive-bombing missions as such were flown. Bombs were carried on some missions during this time but the missions were not actual dive-bombing efforts.

Armed Recon
These were longer-range missions of spotting and breaking up enemy forces. They were designed to help disrupt the German's reinforcement efforts or their retreating movements. These missions were usually flown with bombs which would then be used if targets were found.

Assault Area Patrol

These were similar to area patrols but were flown over the immediate battlefront. Again, bombs were carried most of the time with the pilots instructed to watch for enemy ground targets or aircraft.

Armored Column Cover

Headquarters of the 9th Air Force assigned one group the task of providing continuous cover for one armored column during daylight hours. Each unit was directed to provide 8-12 planes for each column, and as the new flight arrived on station, they checked with the flight being relieved and the ground controller for positions and other pertinent information.

• • •

March 1, 1943

The 363rd Fighter Group was activated on this date at Hamilton Field, California, pursuant to General Order 35 of the 4th Air Force. The new unit, commanded by LtCol. John R. Ulricson, was composed of the 380th, 381st, and 382nd Fighter Squadrons. Assigned to the San Francisco Air Defense Wing, the mission of the 363rd was to act as an Operational Training Unit with P-39 aircraft. Initial personnel were then drawn from the 328th Fighter Group, also based at Hamilton Field.

March 2 - April 8, 1943

After activation, things were in a state of confusion; the Headquarters building was shared with the 357th Fighter Group, which was preparing to move to Tonopah, Nevada. Personnel had to borrow typewriters and paper from the 328th and improvised furniture out of crates and boxes. Then to top everything off, orders were received on March 13 de-activating the Group. Three days later, however, those orders were rescinded. Few officers and enlisted men were assigned to the 363rd early in its history. Activities consisted mainly of lectures, films, drills, and athletics. As for flying, LtCol. Ulricson and Capt. Culberson were forced to borrow planes from the 328th to get in their time. On April 8, Ulricson was sent to the San Francisco Air Defense Wing and Capt. Dave H. Culberson became the new CO. He in turn left for the 328th Fighter Group on April 27, and the 363rd Supply Officer, Maj. Theodore C. Bunker, took command. By the 28th of April, the 363rd had only two officers and five enlisted men.

May 24 - August 1943

On May 24, six pilots and 185 enlisted men arrived at Hamilton Field for assignment to the 363rd. Included were the three squadron CO's: Capt. Evan M. McCall (380th), Capt. Culberson (381st), and Capt. Robert C. McWherter (382nd). Of these three, only McWherter had previous combat experience. He had sailed for the Far East in December of 1941 and flew P-40's in Java with the 17th Pursuit Squadron. While serving here he claimed one victory plus a probable, then escaped to Australia when Java fell. Joining the 35th Fighter Group, McWherter flew P-39's from Australia and New Guinea before returning to the States in late 1942.

Col. Ulricson returned on June 4, and several weeks later, on July 31, the first P-39 "Airacobras" arrived. Three each were assigned to the 380th and 381st while two were sent to the 382nd. August then saw a large number of pilots assigned and training began in earnest.

August 23 - November 6, 1943

August 23 was moving day, as personnel and equipment were sent to Santa Rosa, California. Leaving in convoy at 0800, everyone was at Santa Rosa by mid-afternoon setting up operations. With training intensifying, accidents began to take their toll. On October 3, Lt. Carl L. Kiesig (381st) was killed when he crashed near Tubbs Island during a gunnery flight. On the 21st, three more pilots were involved in accidents: Lt. Donald K. Camden (382nd) died when he hit a mountain four miles south of Hayward; and two 380th fliers were involved in a collision ten miles east of Mount Diable. While Lt. Reinholz escaped with a broken back, Lt. Lawrence Casadont was killed. Back on October 4, the Group began to split-up: the 382nd moved to Hayward, while on the 6th, Headquarters and the 381st moved to Sacramento Municipal Airport, followed by the 380th going to Oakland Municipal Airport on the 8th. Training was rapidly coming to an end, and the last pilot to die in the States was Lt. Glen F. Sanford (380th). He was killed on November 6 when he crashed into San Francisco Bay east of Nichols.

In addition to those pilots killed, a number of other P-39's were written off in accidents during training. Following is a list of those known:

August	17	Lt. Nicholas (380th)	b/o east of Petaluma
September	1	Lt. Ballinger (380th)	c/l Santa Rosa
	7	Lt. McKinney (380th)	b/o southeast of Santa Rosa

	13	Lt. Carter (380th)	b/o northeast of Cotati
	17	Lt. Moyer (381st)	c/l Santa Rosa
	21	Lt. Brink (382nd)	c/l south of Santa Rosa
	22	Lt. Recagno (381st)	c/l Santa Rosa
October	7	Lt. Johnson (380th)	b/o Florence Lake
		Lt. Fryer (380th)	b/o west of Las Vegas
	9	Lt. Steinke (381st)	c/l Phoenix
	25	Lt. Deeds (382nd)	c/l Hayward
November	18	Lt. Monyelle (381st)	b/o Hayward

December 2-December 20, 1943

On December 2, the 363rd loaded into trucks and proceeded to a rail siding in Sacramento, the first step in moving overseas. The train pulled out at 1300 hours heading east, and reached Camp Kilmer, New Jersey, at 1000 hours on December 6. The next week was spent in processing: lectures, inspections, and issuance of gas masks. Then at 0920 on December 14, the 363rd set sail aboard the "Queen Elizabeth", destination: Great Britain. To quote the group diary, "To say the trip was rough would be a misstatement, but to those of us who had never been on the high seas, it seemed the waves were a hundred feet high. Rapidly, most of us wished we were back on terra firma – the more firma the less terra!" Seasickness aside, everyone safely reached Scotland on December 20 and prepared to disembark.

December 21, 1943 - February 1, 1944

Early in the morning of December 21, personnel boarded a train and set out for their new home. At 1000 hours on December 23, the men arrived at Station 471, Keevil, Wiltshire. They were met by the Group's advance echelon (Maj. Cloke, Maj. Thomason, and Capt. McWhirter, the Group Intelligence Officer), and immediately set up quarters and offices. Word was also received that the 363rd would be equipped with P-51 "Mustangs", and everyone looked forward to getting these much vaunted planes. In the meantime, pilots attended lectures while the ground officers went on detached service to other units to study their operations. By January 21, 1944, the 363rd still had no aircraft except for a solitary L-4.

The 363rd's stay at Keevil was short, as on January 22, the Group began to move to Station 166, Rivenhall, Essex. Headquarters and the 382nd made the move on the 22nd, the 381st began on the 30th, while the 380th waited until February 3. The first planes arrived at Rivenhall on January 23 – eleven P-51B's – and flying started the next day. By the 26th, fifteen fighters were on hand, but one was written off in an accident

that day. Lt. Lester F. Aldrich (382nd) taxied into a parked truck, causing heavy damage to both the plane and vehicle.

With the acquisition of the P-51, the 363rd became the second P-51 outfit in the 9th Air Force and third in the European Theater. The 354th Fighter Group had arrived in England during November of 1943 and began operations in December. By the end of February, the 354th already had claimed some 112 kills. The 357th Fighter Group had come to the ETO in November of 1943 and was initially assigned to the 9th Air Force. In late January of 1944, however, it was traded to the 8th Air Force in exchange for the P-47 equipped 358th Fighter Group. The 357th started operations on February 11 and had claimed 21 kills by the end of the month.

February 2 - February 23, 1944

Training with the new planes began immediately, and on February 2, the first overseas fatality occurred. During a cross country flight, Lt. Paul A. Pederson (382nd) crashed into a hill near Burden Hill, Tresham. On February 12, Col. Ulricson had a meeting with all the pilots and as the diary stated, "His talk stressed accidents, the most of which were 'head-up' accidents. He emphasized the fact he didn't care if other groups did have bad records-ours still stunk!" So what happened the next day- everyone went out flying and two planes were cracked up in landings. The ships were flown by a pair of 382nd pilots, Lt. James Watson and Lt. Joe R. Edwards, with Watson's plane being totally demolished.

The Group diary for February 22 also quoted, "Today was one of 'those days'. First we didn't receive instructions on the affiliation mission, so the Colonel plotted a course to take the pilots halfway over the Channel escorting the bombers. Briefing was late and press was late. The Colonel started to take-off and found he had a flat tailwheel. After taxiing off the runway, one of the 382nd pilots plowed into him, tearing up two wings and a horizontal stabilizer. Capt. Culberson took over the Group, which consisted originally of 27 planes. Twenty-five started to take-off and one developed engine trouble and didn't get off, leaving twenty-four. The rest got off just as a snowstorm came up. The planes separated due to the weather, some going over the Channel and some just getting lost. They all came back without mishap, except one who ground looped in landing. What a day!"

February 24, 1944

(#1) LtCol. James H. Howard (currently CO of the 354th Fighter Group) led the 363rd on its first mission of the war. 42 aircraft (12 from the 380th and 15 each from the 381st and 382nd) took off at 1342 for a withdrawal support from the Brussels area. While outbound, three P-51s aborted and the rest made landfall at 1439 near Goedereede. R/V with some B-17's followed near Brussels and these were escorted out safely. The pilots crossed out north of Dunkirk at 1505 and everyone was down by 1520. Two FW-190's were seen near Antwerp by 381st pilots and Lt. Schmidt's 382nd P-51 was hit in the tail by flak, but no serious damage was done.

February 25

(#2) Capt. Jack T. Bradley (another 354th pilot) led 33 P-51s on a withdrawal support from 1045 to 1249. Four Mustangs aborted (one being Lt. Benbenek of the 381st) with the rest crossing in at 1123 north of Cape Gris Nez. The B-17's were picked up west of Amiens at 1138 and were escorted uneventfully until landfall-out north of Calais at 1216.

February 25

(#3) With Capt. Bradley again in the lead, 29 P-51s took off at 1442 on another withdrawal support. Except for seven aborts, the pilots made R/V south of Sedan and both the fighters and bombers crossed out at 1659. The heavies were taken back to England and left near Folkstone with the Mustangs landing back home at 1735.

February 26

The Group flew no mission this day but a 380th Mustang was written-off in a landing accident at Rivenhall. Lt. Earl L. Snyder landed too fast, ran off the runway into the mud, and completely wrecked his plane.

February 29

(#4) LtCol. Howard led 43 Mustangs off for a withdrawal support from 0950 to 1340. All planes made landfall at 1055 north of The Hague with R/V following at 1143. During the mission, Maj. Culberson and Lt. Howell (381st) collided. Culberson suffered damage to a wing while Howell lost part of his vertical tail and rudder. Both men managed to land safely, though Howell was forced to crash-land at Rivenhall. The rest of the 363rd crossed out near Haarlem at 1235 with the planes being down by 1340.

Back home, two more 380th planes were wrecked in training mishaps. Lt. Charles L. Moore cracked-up on landing but was unharmed, while Lt. John E. Molen bailed out near Maldon and his injuries put him in the hospital for several weeks.

March 2

(#5) Capt. Bradley led the Group on a planned escort from 1031 to 1530. 33 P-51s took off with 11 later aborting (380th-2 381st-2, Lts. H. Scott and Miller, 382nd-7). Crossing in at 1110 north of Ostend, the planes reached the R/V point at 1148 but the bombers were never found. Bradley led the P-51s on a patrol of the area until heading out east of Rotterdam at 1415. After returning to England, a 380th Mustang was written off in a landing accident. Lt. Tyler ran out of gas on his final approach to Boxted and safely bellied-in.

March 3

(#6) LtCol. Howard led the 363rd for the last time on a mission from 0942 to 1445. 36 P-51s took off but 11 aborted (380th-6 381st-4, Lts. Gustafson, Mimler, Miller, and McRoberts, 382nd-1) for various reasons. The rest made landfall at 1044 and as they reached the R/V point, near Grabow, the bombers were recalled. The pilots circled the area until 1215 when 30-plus Germans fighters were sighted and engaged. By the time the pilots disengaged at 1235, one enemy plane had been destroyed and several others hit while no P-51s were lost. Lts. Sharrock and Vance (380th) also chased a pair of Ju-88's but broke off when a number of Me-109's arrived on the scene. Landfall-out was from 1340 to 1345 from Ijmuiden to Walcheren. Lt. Brink (382nd) had taken a flak hit near Bremen which knocked out his hydraulics but he returned safely, while Lt. Johnson (380th), who had aborted, bellied-in at Rivenhall without harm.

(1-1-3 air)

Sqn		Claims
381st:	Maj. D.H. Culberson	Me-410 dest(air)
	Lt. E.H. Berglind	Me-109 prob(air)
	Lt. H.D. Knuppel	Me-109 dam(air)
382nd:	Lt. D.L. Boatright	Me-109 dam(air)
	Lt. J.N. Brink	Me-109 dam(air)

March 4

(#7) Maj. Culberson led 33 aircraft up at 1036 for an escort mission. Very bad weather was encountered and eight planes aborted immediately (380th-1, Capt. DeLong; 381st-1, Lt. Spencer; 382nd-6, Lt. Brink, others unknown). The remaining pilots crossed in at 1118 north of Goedereede but shortly afterwards were split-up in the weather. Only Culberson and seven others (Lts. Mimler, McRoberts, Recagno, Howell, Miller, Benbenek, and Carter) reached the R/V point, where a recall was received. Another 381st pilot, Lt. Schmidt, continued alone and made R/V at 1145. He stayed with these bombers until crossing out at 1300 near The Hague. Three 380th pilots, Lts. McEachron, Williams, and Nicholas, R/V'd with a few bombers near Paderborn at 1145. They took them to the Magdeburg area, breaking off at 1245 near Munster, and then crossed out near The Hague at 1315. Three other 380th fliers, Lts. Vance, Reddig, and Hale, made it to the Munster area before they turned for home. Most of the Group was home by 1414, but 11 P-51s (5 from the 381st and 6 from the 382nd) failed to return. Evidently all were lost in collisions or disorientation in the clouds, as several other pilots spun-out in the haze but effected recovery. Lost were Lt. Louis Moyer, Lt. Victor G. Gustafson, Lt. Theodore D. Owings, Lt. Leonard H. Polley, and Lt. Burr H. Sullivan of the 381st, and Lt. Lester F. Aldrich, Lt. Joe R. Edwards, F/O Willie D. Collins, Lt. Wilbur E. McGee, Lt. John H. Theil, and Lt. James E. Watson of the 382nd.

(11 losses)

Stories over the years have stated that these losses were due to enemy fighters, but descriptions from surviving pilots and lack of radio activity indicating a fight, lead to the conclusion the losses were due to lack of proper instrument training in adverse weather conditions.

March 5
(#8) Col. Ulricson led 29 planes on a long-range mission to Bordeaux from 1010 to 1415. Two 381st pilots aborted (Lts. Carter and Gallagher) but the rest crossed in at 1100 near Trouville. The Mustangs reached the R/V point at 1150 but the bombers were never sighted. After circling the area without incident, the ships headed home, crossing out near Caen at 1300

March 8
(#9) Col. Ulricson led 48 P-51s on an escort to the Berlin area from 1102 to 1652. Twelve planes aborted (380th-4 381st-5, Maj. Culberson, Lts. Jacobs, Smith, Webb, and Johnson, 382nd-3) and the rest made landfall at 1215 near Ijmuiden. R/V was made west of Celle at 1311 and the bombers were taken to targets around Berlin. 15-plus enemy fighters were engaged near the city with 363rd pilots destroying two and Lt. Frank Q. O'Connor (of the 354th Fighter Group and lending a hand flying with the 380th Fighter Squadron this day) downed two more. Lt. Neill F. Ullo (380th) was last seen in the fight with his Mustang disintegrating near Berlin and fortunately he escaped to become a prisoner. On the way home, Lt. Smith (381st) strafed in the Calais area and damaged a flak tower. The rest of

the Group later crossed out at 1625 near Boulogne and Lt. Hill (380th) crash-landed at Rivenhall but suffered no injuries.

(2-0-0 air)

(1 lost)

Sqn		Claims
380th:	F/O B.W. Carr	Me-109 dest(air)
381st:	Lt. H.R. Howell	Me-109 dest(air)

March 9
(#10) Maj. Culberson led an escort to Neinburg from 1003 to 1430. Six P-51s aborted (380th-1 381st-2, Lts. H. Scott and Spencer, 382nd-3, Lt. Brink was one) but the rest made landfall near The Hague, followed by R/V east of Celle at 1154. The bombers were taken to Neinburg without problem then left at 1319 near Rathenow. All pilots (except five) crossed out at 1350 near The Hague. Earlier, part of the 382nd became separated and two pilots finished the mission with the 4th Fighter Group while three more hooked up with the 354th.

According to the group diary, "Another 'milk run' today – and Jerry wouldn't or couldn't – and didn't come up to fight. Again, it was a case of no runs, no hits, no errors"

March 10-17
The 363rd stood down for the week for maintenance and training. There were missions scheduled on two days but weather factors led to them being scrubbed. On the 14th, Maj. Irvin (HdQts), Maj. McCall, Lt. Nicholas (380th), Lt. Mimler, Lt. Miller (381st), and Lt. Thompson (382nd) along with a complement of enlisted men, were sent to Milfield to attend an air support school. The men would later return on April 1.

March 18
(#11) Maj. Culberson led 47 P-51s off at 1133 for the day's mission. The planes were eight miles from landfall when they were recalled and all landed by 1300.

(#12) Maj. Culberson led the second mission from 1428 to 1745. 35 planes took off (Two 382nd pilots, Lts. Kunz and Coble later aborted) and made landfall at 1511 near Dunkirk. R/V was made at 1545 near Vitrey and the bombers were taken out to Le Treport at 1707 and left in mid-Channel at 1717. On the way home, the P-51 of Lt. Elmo H. Berglind (381st) was seen to smoke then later catch fire. Berglind was forced to bail out over France where he evaded capture and returned to England a few months later.

(1 lost)

March 20

(#13) Col. Ulricson led a mission from 1008 to 1330. 43 aircraft took off (two later turned back, F/O Scott, 381st and Lt. Asbury, 382nd) and made landfall at 1048 near Ostend. At the R/V point the bombers were recalled due to a solid wall of cloud and a few stragglers were escorted out. Several pilots dropped down to strafe on the way home with Lt. Howell (381st) destroying a loco near Namur and another near Valenciennes, while Lt. Brink (382nd) destroyed a third loco near Senarport. Lt. Robert E. Spencer and Lt. Daren L. Benbenek (381st) were lost for unknown reasons and the remaining fliers crossed out at 1240 near Dieppe.

(2 lost)

March 21

Due to the weather, the 363rd stood down for maintenance and training. While on a practice flight, Lt. Stewart P. Sullivan and Lt. Edwin G. Watkins (382nd) collided during a cross-over. One pilot was killed instantly while the second bailed out too low for his chute to open.

(2 killed)

March 22

(#14) Lt. Tilson led 12 P-51s of the 380th on a mission from 0838 to 1223. Four planes aborted and the rest crossed in at 0938 over Texel Island. No R/V was made but a few stragglers were escorted out. Some pilots strafed on the way home with Lt. Hale claiming 0-1 machine gun nest. The planes later crossed out from 1140 to 1145 over Walcheren Island.

March 22

(#15) Col. Ulricson led 36 P-51s on a withdrawal support from 1026 to 1530. Three planes aborted (380th-2 381st-1, Lt. Schmidt) and the rest made landfall at 1133 over Texel Island. R/V was accomplished at 1320 near Berlin and the fighters and bombers later crossed out at 1449 near Chagen. The heavies were then left in mid-Channel at 1459 as the 363rd headed for Rivenhall.

March 23

(#16) Lt. Schmidt led 35 planes on a mission from 0833 to 1200. Almost half (15) of the planes aborted (380th-4, Lts. Kammerlohr, McKinney, Clough, and Clemovitz; 381st-5, Lts. Jacobs, H. Scott, McRoberts, Smith, and Howell; 382nd-6) and the rest made landfall at 0941 near Den Helder. R/V with some B-24's followed at 1012 in the Quackenbruck area, the bombers were taken to their targets and out, then were left at 1124 near Walcheren.

March 24

(#17) Col. Ulricson led a withdrawal support from 0934 to 1200. 40 pilots took off (three later aborted, Lts. Bruce and Tilson, 380th, and Lt. H. Scott, 381st) and made landfall at 1030 over the Hook of Holland. R/V was at 1047 near Brussels and the bombers were taken out without incident. Two other P-51s had been scheduled to go on the mission but an accident washed them out. Lt. Hale and Lt. Vance (380th) collided while taxiing, causing damage to each ship.

March 25

Another day of release and a pilot was killed on a training flight. While practicing dive-bombing, Lt. Newman E. Tyree (381st) lost the tail of his P-51 and crashed into Holbrook Bay.

(1 killed)

March 26

(#18) Col. Ulricson led a dive-bombing mission from 1330 to 1600. 48 P-51s took off (with Lt. McKinney and F/O Diya, 380th, aborting) and crossed in at 1414 near Ault. The pilots dive-bombed in the Creil area with poor results then crossed out at 1505 near the Somme River.

March 29

The 363rd was released due to weather and another pilot died in an accident. Lt. Thomas E. Hale (380th) was on a visit to a B-17 base at Grafton Underwood and upon leaving he gave the field a buzz-job. He pulled straight up, then fell off, hit the ground in an apparently good belly-landing, but then was killed when the Mustang exploded.

(1 killed)

March 30

Another down day and the accident rate continued to take a toll. Lt. George F. Parker (382nd) died when his P-51 crashed into Holbrook Bay due to mechanical failure.

(1 killed)

Also on this date, Maj. Marshall Cloke took over as CO of the 380th, replacing Maj. McCall, who stayed on as the Squadron's Operations Officer. According to the 380th diary, "Our accident rate has been exceedingly high and the change has been made in an apparent attempt to correct the situation." This seems a bit strange, considering that McCall had been at Milfield for two weeks prior to this. Also, the 380th's accident rate was no worse, or better, than either the 381st or 382nd. Regardless, West Point graduate Cloke became the new commander. Filling Cloke's position as Deputy Group CO was Maj. Ben S. Irvin, a combat veteran of both the Pacific and European Theaters. Flying with the 17th Pursuit Squadron in Java, Irvin claimed two kills against the Japanese. Coming home from the Pacific, he later went to Europe as a Squadron CO in the P-47 equipped 362nd Fighter Group, then was transferred to the 363rd in early March

April 1

(#19) Col. Ulricson led 54 P-51s on a withdrawal support from 0810 to 1406. Eleven planes aborted (Lts. Benson, Clough, Clemovitz, Ray, Tyler, Reddig, and McKinney, 380th; Lts. Wood, McRoberts, and Jacobs, 381st; T/Sgt. Hare, 382nd) and the rest crossed in at 0900 south of Ostend. The pilots circled the R/V area until hooking up with the bombers at 1015 near Baden. Escort was given to the Laon area where the Mustangs broke at 1220. Landfall-out later followed east of Calais at 1310. Just prior to R/V the 380th was bounced by some Me-109's but no damage was done. Then near Lake Constance, Lt. Owen (380th) bounced a pair of Me-109's and hit two. A pair of 381st pilots strafed an airfield near Luxembourg and shot up a quartet of enemy planes, plus Lt. Jacobs (381st) destroyed a barrage balloon ten miles west of Ostend.

(0-1-1 air)

(0-4 ground)

Sqn		Claims
380th:	Lt. A.W. Owen	Me-109 prob(air)
		Me-109 dam(air)
381st:	Lt. W.R. Schmidt	(2)u/i a/c dam(grd)
	Lt. L.D. Smutz	(2)u/i a/c dam(grd)

April 5

(#20) Maj. Culberson led 53 aircraft up for a strafing sweep from 1320 to 1457. Six P-51s aborted (380th-1 381st-3, Lts. Ringgenberg, Stuart, and H. Scott, 382nd-2) and the rest crossed in near St. Valery at 1408. The original mission was planned to strafe Tours/Laval, but bad weather forced the Group to look elsewhere. Tricqueville was attacked and while Lt. Donald M. Lewis (382nd) was lost, two German planes were hit and other claims were for 0-2 hangars, 0-3 flak towers, and 0-2 buildings. Lewis, who bailed out near the field, managed to evade

capture and returned to Allied control in August.

(1-1 ground)

(1 lost)

Sqn		Claims
381st:	Lt. A.M. Mimler	He-111 dest(grd)
	Lt. W.R. Schmidt	Ju-88 dam(grd)

April 8

(#21) Maj. McWherter led the Group on an escort from 1141 to 1535. Out of 54 planes which took off, 15 aborted (380th-5, Maj. McCall, Lts. Bruce, Owen, Clough, and F/O Diya; 381st-4, Lts. McRoberts, H. Scott, Webb, and F/O G. Scott; 382nd-6) and the rest crossed in at 1240 near Ijmuiden. R/V followed at 1300 north of Lingen, then near Wittengen, 40-plus Luftwaffe fighters were engaged. Pilots claimed 7 victories while Lt. Alfred Fontes (380th) and Lt. John A. Wenner (382nd) were both downed near Gardelegen. After the fights, the 363rd left the bombers near Zwolle and crossed out over Ijmuiden. Reaching England, two 381st pilots crash-landed; Lt. Wood at Sudbury and Lt. Thoresz at Woodbridge.

(7-1-6 air)

(2 lost)

Sqn		Claims
HdQts:	Maj. B.S. Irvin	FW-190 dam(air)
380th:	Lt. C.R. Reddig	Me-109 dest(air)
	Lt. J.A. Sharrock	(1.5)FW-190 dam(air)
	Lt. N.D. Hersberger	(.5)FW-190 dam(air)
381st:	Lt. W.R. Schmidt	FW-190 dest(air)
		Bu-181 dest(air)
	Maj. D.H. Culberson	FW-190 dest(air)
		(2)FW-190 dam(air)
	Lt. J.M. Boland	Me-109 dest(air)
	Lt. J.B. Dalglish	Me-109 dest(air)
	Lt. W.W. Steinke	FW-190 dest(air)
	Lt. A.M. Mimler	FW-190 prob(air)
	Lt. R.P. Lucas	FW-190 dam(air)

April 9

(#22) Maj. Irvin led 47 planes on a withdrawal support from 1304 to 1830. The pilots (minus ten aborts, 380th-1, Lt. Ballinger; 381st-1, Lt. Williams; 382nd-8) crossed in at 1450 near Sylt and made R/V at 1545 in the Wandrup area. The bombers were escorted out and left at 1645 over the North Sea. Two fliers failed to return as Lt. William W. Steinke (381st) crashed near Ameland Island and Lt. Ben A. Pollard (382nd) crashed into the sea off Tessel Island.

(2 lost)

April 10

(#23) Col. Ulricson led 47 P-51s on a dive-bombing mission from 1000 to 1215. The planes crossed in at 1040 over Nieuwe Sluis and arrived at the Hasselt marshalling yards at 1100. At least one loco received a direct hit (from Ulricson's bomb) before the planes departed and crossed out at 1133 over Nieuwe Sluis.

April 10

(#24) 46 Mustangs (13 of which later aborted) took off at 1720 for an escort to the Namur area. The planes crossed in at 1755 near Furness and R/V'd with some B-26's shortly after, at 1800. After leaving the bombers the pilots made landfall-out at 1905 near Ostend and everyone was down by 1940.

April 11

(#25) Col. Ulricson led 53 P-51s on a mission from 0912 to 1505. Six planes aborted and the rest made landfall at 1006 near Haarlem. R/V followed near Streyersburg at 1050 and the bombers were later left at 1230 near Crossens and the Group crossed out at 1422 over the Hook of Holland. During the mission, a number of Germans were encountered near Schonebeck and Magdeburg with 3 kills recorded. Several pilots also strafed in the Elbe area on the way out and shot up a number of grounded planes. Lt. Don Boatright (382nd) was wounded in the eye by shrapnel but after patching himself up, flew back to Rivenhall, and made a normal landing . Lt. James B. McKenna (380th) was radio-relay and he simply disappeared over the Channel. One of the pilots aborting was Maj. McWherter (382nd). Turning back with a rough engine, he was bounced twice by a P-51 coded VF-T of the 4th Fighter Group. This Mustang finally broke off after Lt. Brown made two passes to get it off McWherter's tail.

(3-0-2 air)
(2-4 ground)
(1 lost)

Sqn		Claims
380th:	Lt. A.W. Owen	Me-109 dest(air)
		(2)Me-109 dam(air)
	Lt. J.A. Sharrock	Me-109 dest(air)
381st:	Lt. H.R. Howell	Me-109 dest(air)

	Lt. A.J. Reinhart	He-111 dam(grd)
382nd:	Lt. D.H. Rook	He-177 dest(grd)
		Ju-88 dam(grd)
	Lt. D.L. Boatright	He-177 dest(grd)
	Lt. F. Kozaczka	He-177 dam(grd)
	Lt. R.E. Schillereff	He-177 dam(grd)

April 11

(#26) 49 P-51s (11 of which later aborted) flew an escort from 1712 to 1927. R/V was made between Dunkirk and Ostend and the bombers were taken to the Halle area and back out without incident.

April 12

(#27) Lt. Thompson led 46 planes on an escort from 1209 to 1620. Eleven pilots aborted, including the original mission leader, Maj. McCall (380th-3 381st-5, Maj. Culberson, Lts. Mimler, McRoberts, Webb, and Henry, 382nd-3). The Mustangs crossed in at 1300 near Knocke but no R/V was made and the squadrons became separated in bad weather. Lt. Harry R. Howell (381st) suffered mechanical problems and bailed out near Magdeburg to become a prisoner. The remaining P-51s crossed out from Egmond to Cuxhaven at 1550.

(1 lost)

April 13

(#28) Col. Ulricson led 49 planes on a withdrawal support from the Halle area from 1213 to 1702. Nine pilots aborted (381st-3, Lts. Boland, Johnson, and Henry, 382nd-6, one was Lt. Brink) and the rest made landfall at 1305 near Ostend. Seven FW-190's were seen near Trier but these avoided contact. R/V was at 1405 near Saarbrucken and later, in the vicinity of Halle, German fighters were encountered. One Me-109 was downed here by the 381st while a 382nd pilot nailed a second northeast of Stuttgart. The bombers were left over Luxembourg at 1615 and everyone crossed out at 1710 near Dunkirk.

(2-0-0 air)

Sqn		Claims
381st:	Lt. W.R. Schmidt	Me-109 dest(air)
382nd:	Lt. R.B. McGee	Me-109 dest(air)

April 14

To quote the Group diary, "This was the big moving day for the 363rd. We packed up bag and headed for the sunny southland. Some went by truck, some by jeep, and some by rail. Upon reaching Staplehurst, Kent, it started to rain. The advance party had set up tents ready for us in an apple orchard by the side of a grass field. The orchard became quarters and the field became the strip. An old, rather broken-down farmhouse, constructed in 1719, is headquarters. Immediately upon arriving, everyone started to work, setting up operations and intelligence trailers, wall tents, etc. A hot supper was ready by 6 p.m. and the 363rd in full strength hit the line like old-time chow hounds. The mess tables were in the open, under the trees, very picturesque and Al Fresio, but wet under feet and under seat. Incidentally, the cots failed to arrive so the 363rd slept on the ground, muttering into the evening, 'It's rough in the ETO'".

April 15
(#29) Maj. Irvin led 40 aircraft on a planned escort from 1202 to 1335. Three planes aborted (381st-1 382nd-2) and of the rest, only a few reached Dummer Lake due to solid overcast from England across to the Continent. Over the Channel, both Lt. Edward F. Cahill and T/Sgt. Clifford W. Hare (382nd) spun-in and were killed. Lt. Samuel McRoberts (381st) died when he crashed into a hill while trying to land at Detling, and Lt. Ringgenberg (381st) spun out over the Channel but managed to bail out. He was fortunate, as having lost both his Mae West and dinghy, he was picked up by a fishing boat. Ringgenberg, by the way, could not swim!

(4 lost)

Also on this day, another pilot was lost in action but not while on a mission with the 363rd. Lt. Robert E. Coble (382nd) had been on detached service with the 15th Air Force in Italy studying ground support operations. While on a mission, Coble was downed by flak and captured, the only Group pilot thus lost. Others known to have been sent to Italy were Maj. Thomason (Hdqts), who went from January 17 until early February, and Maj. Cloke (380th), and Lts. Carter and Knuppel (381st). The latter went with Coble in late March and returned to England in early April.

(1 lost)

April 18
(#30) Maj Irvin led the 44 P-51s on an escort to the Berlin area from 1143 to 1640. Landfall (minus nine aborts, 380th-6 381st-1, Lt. Dalglish, 382nd-2) was at 1258 north of Ijmuiden, with R/V at 1358 near Ratzeburg. The bombers were taken to their targets then left at 1506 southwest of Hamburg. On the way home, Lt. Johnson and Lt. Smutz (381st) strafed in the Einbeck area and claimed 2-0 locos. The planes later crossed out at 1550 north of Ijmuiden.

From the 382nd diary, "It was the usual milk run – no hits, no runs, no errors. Our squadron seems to be having difficulty finding any Jerries who want to fight."

April 19
(#31) Col. Ulricson led 46 P-51s (three of which aborted, 381st-1, Lt. Vesely, 382nd-2) on a dive-bombing mission from 1401 to 1730. The Group arrived at Hasselt at 1520 and two squadrons bombed while the third flew cover. Several hits were scored on the tracks and among the buildings of the yard before the Mustangs headed home.

April 22
(#32) Maj. Irvin led 46 planes (F/O Scott, 381st, later aborted) on a dive-bombing mission from 1102 to 1259. The planes crossed in at 1140 north of Dunkirk and reached the marshalling yard at Malines at 1158. Twenty P-51s flew top cover while the rest bombed-scoring hits on buildings and oil storage tanks. Everyone later crossed out at 1230 north of Dunkirk.

April 22
(#33) Col. Ulricson led 49 P-51s on a sweep from 1626 to 2030. One Mustang turned back (F/O Carr, 380th) and the rest crossed in at 1710 near Cayeaux with the squadrons then splitting up. The 380th swept the Karlsruhe area and claimed 2-1 locos near Druschel and Braben (all shared by Lts. Hersberger, Kellogg, and Sharrock, and F/O Diya) and 2-3 boats (2-1 shared by Maj. Cloke and Lts. Ray, Nicholas, and Snyder, and 0-2 shared by Lts. Tilson, Bruce, Maxwell, and Benson) while Lt. Paul R. Maxwell and Lt. John A. Sharrock were lost. Maxwell was hit by flak and bailed out near Speyer while Sharrock bailed out in the Germersheim-Graben area after a flak hit. The 381st swept Bad Kreuznach and claimed 0-1 warehouse on the airfield at Spa. Two pilots were also lost-Lt. Ward F. Miller bailed out near Ludwigshafen due to flak damage and Capt. George R. Doerr had to bail out near St. Dizier. The 382nd swept the Frankfurt area, strafing both Griesheim and Ingelheim airfields, claiming 0-4 planes, 1-0 flak tower, 0-1 loco, and 0-3 buildings.

(0-4 ground)
(4 lost)

Sqn		Claims
382nd:	Lt. L.E. Webster	u/i a/c dam(grd)
		glider dam(grd)

| Capt. L.D. Morrison | Ju-88 dam(grd) |
| Lt. J. Robertson | Ju-88 dam(grd) |

April 23
(#34) Col. Ulricson led 51 planes on a dive-bombing mission from 1139 to 1351. Two pilots aborted and the rest crossed in at 1207 near Gravelines. The Mustangs arrived at the Namur marshalling yards at 1235 and two squadrons bombed. A few hits were scored on warehouses and sheds then the Group crossed out at 1315 near Gravelines.

April 23
(#35) Maj. Cloke led 50 planes (one 380th flier aborted) on a sweep from 1557 to 1930. The pilots made landfall at 1713 near Den Helder then swept the Bremen area from 1740 to 1755. The 380th strafed buildings, trucks, and construction equipment at Oosterwalde Airfield but Lt. James E. Barlow was downed by flak. The remaining men crossed out from 1827 to 1905 between Den Helder and Zand Voort.
(1 lost)

April 24
(#36) Col. Ulricson led 52 planes on an escort from 1124 to 1624. Minus eight aborts, (380th-4 382nd-4) the P-51s crossed in at 1208 over Bourg and R/V came at 1305. The bombers were taken to targets south of Augsburg and later left south of Neustadt at 1430. Landfall-out then was made at 1610 from Bourg to Calais.

April 25
(#37) Maj. Irvin led 49 P-51s on a sweep from 0725 to 1230. 40 P-51s crossed in (nine aborted, 381st-5, Lts. Davis, Henry, Johnson, Kennedy, and Vesely, 382nd-4) at 0758 near Coxyde, arrived in their assigned area at 0940, then split up to sweep. Ten boxes of B-24's were also picked up west of Bockingen at 1000 then left at 1020 southwest of Parmasens. Two Me-109's were seen near the bombers but they dove into the overcast before anyone could reach them. Also, flak hit the P-51 of Lt. Schmidt, and as the Group diary stated, "Lt. Schmidt of the 382nd caught a large shell in his right wing. It severed the main spar, took his outboard gun with it, and left him with only a wing and a prayer. That's enough for a pilot of this Group and Schmidt brought his plane back with an excellent landing."

April 26
The 363rd was released for maintenance and training. While on a practice dive-bombing flight, the 382nd P-51s of Lt. Fred B. Deeds and Lt. Edward T. Pawlak collided. Fortunately, both pilots bailed out and were rescued by fishing boats.

April 27
(#38) Col. Ulricson led 45 P-51s on a dive-bombing mission from 1034 to 1232. The Group crossed in at 1120 near Blankenburg and arrived at the Charleroi marshaling yards at 1129. Due to bad weather, the pilots proceeded to Eckloo, Maldegen, and Bruges Airfields and several buildings and hangars were damaged. Landfall-out later came at 1214 near Blankenburg.

April 27
(#39) 46 P-51s flew a dive-bombing mission from 1634 to 1825. One aircraft aborted (Lt. H. Scott-381st) and the rest crossed in at 1715 near Dieppe. The Mustangs arrived at the Nantes-Gassicourt marshaling yards at 1730 and scored hits on the engine sheds, tracks, and buildings. Six 382nd pilots also strafed Illiers Airfield claiming 0-1 flak tower and 0-1 hangar. Everyone later crossed out at 1756 near Fecamp.

April 28
(#40) With Col. Ulricson in the lead, 44 aircraft flew a dive-bombing mission from 0815 to 1040. Lt. Henry (381st) turned back while the rest made landfall at 0900 near St. Valery. The Group was originally to hit the airfield at Laon/Athies, but clouds prevented an attack. The 380th then bombed Coulomiere Airfield, hitting some buildings and the runway. The 381st attacked Le Bourget, damaging several hangars, and Lt. Brink's 382nd flight strafed on the way home claiming 0-1 flak tower and 0-1 radio tower, both northwest of Pontoise. All Mustangs then crossed out at 1020 north of Dieppe.

April 29
(#41) Maj. Irvin led 51 planes on an escort from 0838 to 1345. Seven pilots aborted (380th-4 381st-3, Lts. Stuart, Johnson, and Henry) and the rest crossed in at 0950 and made R/V at 1020 near Dummer Lake. The bombers were taken to the Berlin area and later left near Gifhorn at 1215. Lt. Smith and Lt. Tucker (381st) strafed from Lewe to Recklinghausen, claiming 7-0 locos, 1-0 vehicle, and a He-115 damaged. Due to a briefing error, all four planes of the 380th's "A" Flight ran out of fuel near Redon, with Lt. Norman D. Hersberger, Lt. Albert

G. Johnson, Lt. Arthur W. Owen, and F/O Daniel G. Diya all bailing out. The remainder of the P-51s crossed out at 1320 near Walcheren.

(0-1 ground)
(4 lost)

Sqn		Claims
381st:	Lt. C.H. Smith	He-115 dam(grd)

April 30

(#42) Maj. Culberson led 53 planes (two later aborted, one each from the 380th, Lt. Clemovitz, and 382nd) on an escort from 0824 to 1315. The pilots crossed in at 0900 near Le Treport and made R/V at 0944 near Sancerre. The bombers were taken to the Leipzig area and then left at 1102 near Roanne. North of Montargis, four Me-109's bounced the heavies and the 380th broke up their attack and downed one Messerschmitt. Lt. Charles L. Moore (380th) suffered a coolant loss and bailed out near Mayenne but evaded capture and returned to Allied hands in August. The rest of the Group crossed out at 1218 near Cabourg.

(1-0-0 air)
(1 lost)

Sqn		Claims
380th:	Lt. G.T. McEachron	Me-109 dest(air)

May 1

(#43) Col. Ulricson led 42 P-51s on a dive-bombing mission from 0919 to 1117. Two 380th planes aborted (one being Maj. McCall) while the rest made landfall at 0952 near Gravelines. The Namur marshalling yards were attacked with hits scored on buildings and tracks. One flight also swept south to Florennes afterwards and crossed out at 1055 near Gravelines while the other pilots crossed out over Knocke at 1046.

(#44) Maj. Irvin led the 363rd on a dive-bombing mission from 1750 to 1905. All 44 planes crossed in near Hardelot at 1821 and the Waurin marshaling yards were hit with good results. Lt. Ross S. Sykes (382nd) was hit by flak and his P-51 exploded over the target and the rest of the planes crossed out at 1848 near Wimereux.

(1 lost)

May 2

(#45) 42 P-51s (two of which later aborted) flew a dive-bombing mission from 1120 to 1317. The planes crossed in at 1155

near Furness then attacked the marshalling yards at Namur with poor results. One flight also strafed the airfield at Tirlemont-Gossencourt where Lt. Robertson shot up an aircraft and Lt. Brink damaged a flak tower. Everyone later crossed out at 1258 near Furness and after reaching England, Lt. Harold Scott (381st) crash-landed but escaped injury.

(0-1 ground)

Sqn		Claims
382nd:	Lt. J. Robertson	Me-109 dam(grd)

May 4

(#46) With Col. Ulricson in the lead, 52 P-51s flew an escort from 0838 to 1215. Except for seven aborts (380th-3 381st-2, Lts. Davis and Kennedy, 382nd-2), the Group crossed in at 0941 near Ijmuiden. Shortly after R/V at 1015 near Salzwedel, the mission was scrubbed. On the way out, Lt. Brown (382nd) strafed, claiming 2-0 locos and 0-3 barges, while Lt. Williams (380th) damaged a third loco near Heldersheim. A Me-109 was also seen but it dove into the overcast before any P-51s arrived. The planes crossed out at 1115 near Schouwen and after returning, F/O Carr (380th) had an engine fire and he bailed out southwest of Manston.

May 6

(#47) Lt. Brown led 8 P-51s of the 382nd on a sweep from 1930 to 2100. Landfall was in the Seine area and the pilots then circled for ten minutes. Everyone then crossed out at 2020 west of Le Havre after an uneventful trip.

May 7

(#48) Maj. Cloke led an escort from 0829 to 1330. 51 planes took off but 13 aborted (380th-6 381st-3, Maj. Culberson, Lt. Freyermuth, and F/O G. Scott, 382nd-4) and the remainder crossed in at 0907 in heavy overcast. R/V was accomplished at 1045 near Wittenburg and the bombers were left near Dummer Lake at 1204. Landfall-out was then made near Den Helder at 1314.

May 8

(#49) Maj. Irvin led 50 P-51s on a withdrawal support from 0824 to 1246. Seven pilots aborted (380th-4 381st-2, Lts. Jacobson and Gallagher, 382nd-1) and the rest made landfall at 0942 near Egmond. No R/V was made as the bombers turned back at Muritz Lake at 1115. The 380th found four boxes of B-24's near Vechta at 1100 and took them out; the 382nd picked up twelve boxes south of Bremen at 1030; and the 381st found a single B-17 and escorted him out. The Group later crossed out at 1215 in the Egmond area.

The 380th diary for this date stated, "Jerry may still be fighting but he certainly hasn't put up much of a showing as far as this particular squadron is concerned."

May 9

(#50) Maj. Irvin led 51 planes up at 0751 for an escort. Only one pilot aborted and the others crossed in at 0835 near Nieuport. R/V with some B-24's followed at 0901 in the St. Hubert area and the bombers were taken to Liege and left there. Crossing out, the last plane was back at Staplehurst by 1100.

(#51) Lt. Brink led 8 P-51s of the 382nd on a sweep from 1450 to 1713. The pilots crossed in at 1514 near Cayeaux and strafed in the Creil area from 1630. Two Fw-190's and a motorcycle were damaged before the pilots crossed out at 1650 near Cayeaux.

(0-2 ground)

Sqn		Claims
382nd:	Lt. J. Robertson	(2)FW-190 dam(grd)

Two days earlier, the 363rd had undergone a command change. Col. John Ulricson was moved to a job at 9th Air Force Headquarters and was replaced as CO by LtCol. James B. Tipton. A veteran of the European war, Tipton had come overseas as Deputy CO of the 366th Fighter Group, a 9th Air Force P-47 outfit. To quote the group diary, "It is difficult to express the feelings of all of us in losing 'Honest John' as CO, but let it be said he was a good officer, a good pilot, and a good friend to all of us."

The 382nd diary had this to say, "Late tonight, the new group commander, LtCol. Tipton, inspected troops of all squadrons on the runway strip in front of the Headquarters buildings. After a dry-run parade, the men passed in review, then formed for inspection. Immediately after inspection, he addressed the entire group, announced its aims in administration and operation, and promised a more rigid discipline to everyone in his command." One thing to keep in mind is the fact that just days before, King Peter of Yugoslavia and other dignitaries had visited the field. A number of men failed to salute the official cars, and as a result, the whole post was restricted as a disciplinary measure. Throughout the group and squadron diaries, mention is often made of inspections which proved to be unsatisfactory for various reasons and a general lack of mili-

tary discipline. This pattern started in the States during training and continued up to the end of the 363rd's life as a fighter group. Whether Ulricson was replaced just because of this fact, however, is unfair assumption. During the war, Group Commanders in both the 8th and 9th Air Forces (as well as in other Theaters) were changed with regularity for a number of reasons.

May 11

(#52) Maj. Irvin led 52 aircraft on an escort from 1706 to 2010. Two 380th P-51's aborted and the rest made landfall at 1747 near Furness. R/V came at 1810 in the Namur area and the bombers were taken to Trier. Three Me-109's were engaged in the target area and one was probably destroyed. Then near Marches, eight more Me-109's bounced the 380th and shot down Lt. Roy Benson and Lt. Lloyd M. Bruce. The bombers were later left near Furness at 2025 as the planes crossed out.

(0-1-0 air)

(2 lost)

Sqn		Claims
381st:	Lt. A.M. Mimler	Me-109 prob(air)

May 12

(#53) Maj. Irvin led 50 P-51s on a penetration-target-withdrawal support from 1054 to 1600. Five Mustangs turned back (380th-2 381st-2, Lts. Johnson and Thoresz, 382nd-1) and the remainder crossed in at 1139 near Furness. R/V followed at 1230 near Frankfurt, the bombers were taken through their targets and back out, being left at Frankfurt at 1430. At 1427, the 381st ran into six fighters near Witzlar and damaged one. Then some pilots strafed an airfield in the area and Lts. Smith and Tucker also claimed 0-1 loco. The Group later made landfall-out at 1520 in the Furness area.

(0-0-1 air)

(2-9 ground)

Sqn		Claims
381st:	Lt. J.M. Boland	Me-109 dam(air)
	Lt. C.H. Smith	(.5)Me-109 dest(grd)
		(.5)FW-200 dest(grd)
		(4)He-111 dam(grd)
		FW-190 dam(grd)
	Lt. D.R. Tucker	(.5)Me-109 dest(grd)
		(.5)FW-200 dest(grd)
		(4)He-111 dam(grd)

May 13

(#54) Maj. Cloke led 51 planes up for an escort from 1152 to 1615. Four pilots aborted (two each by the 380th and 382nd, Lts. R. McGee and Ladas) and the rest made landfall at 1333 near Busum. R/V came at 1335 near Albersdorf and while en route to Tutow, Cloke heard of a big fight near Nahe and he led the Group there. 20-plus Germans were engaged and one was destroyed and after the fight, the squadrons split up. The 380th stayed with the bombers, later left them at 1512 near Nusted, and crossed out at 1532 near St. Peter. The 381st and 382nd strafed airfields at Barth, Stade, Schwaan, Groszenborde, and Eckenforder Bay, claiming 15 destroyed, plus Lts. Schmidt, Davis, Freyermuth, and Shea (381st) claimed 0-2 trucks and 0-1 hangar.

(1-0-3 air)

(15-27 ground)

Sqn		Claims
380th:	Maj. M. Cloke	FW-190 dest(air)
	Lt. B.R. Williams	(2)FW-190 dam(air)
381st:	Lt. R.D. Freyermuth	(3)Trainer dest(grd)
		(.25)He-111 dest(grd)
		(3.75)Trainer dam(grd)
		(.75)He-111 dam(grd)
	Lt. C.H. Davis	Trainer dest(grd)
		(.25)He-111 dest(grd)
		(3.75)Trainer dam(grd)
		(.75)He-111 dam(grd)
	Lt. W.R. Schmidt	Trainer dest(grd)
		(.25)He-111 dest(grd)
		(3.75)Trainer dam(grd)
		(.75)He-111 dam(grd)
	Lt. C.E. Shea	(.25)He-111 dest(grd)
		(3.75)Trainer dam(grd)
		(.75)He-111 dam(grd)
382nd:	Lt. M.A. Thompson	FW-190 dam(air)
	Lt. J.R. Brown	He-111 dest(grd)
		Me-110 dest(grd)
		BV-222 dest(grd)
		(3)He-115 dam(grd)
		Me-109 dam(grd)
	Lt. R.E. Schillereff	(2)Ju-88 dest(grd)
	Lt. W.E. Bullard	Ju-88 dest(grd)
		Ju-88 dam(grd)
	Lt. E.W. Odell	Ju-88 dest(grd)
	Lt. W.H. Steiner	Ju-88 dest(grd)
	Lt. J.R. Stricker	(2)Ju-88 dam(grd)
		Me-109 dest(grd)
		He-111 dam(grd)
	Lt. F. Kozaczka	u/i a/c dam(grd)

May 17

(#55) Lts. Brink and Robertson of the 382nd flew a Type-16 control from 1515 to 1755. The planes crossed in at 1535 near Dieppe and proceeded to Creil. They then turned northwest to Laon, southwest to Beaumont Oise, southwest to St. Andre L'Eure, then to Conches and finally to the north. The pair claimed 0-1 flak tower before making landfall at 1730 west of Dieppe.

May 19

(#56) Maj. Irvin led 53 planes (three from the 380th aborted) on an escort from 1145 to 1705. The Group crossed in at 1250 near Ijmuiden and made R/V in the Templin area at 1420. 15-plus FW-190's were seen over Kiel Bay and two were destroyed by the 380th. Near Waabs, 4 FW-190's were bounced by the 381st and a third Focke Wulf was shot down and one more damaged, then a second 190 was damaged near Langerland by T/Sgt. Yochim. Lt. Smith (381st) also strafed Husum and Jagel Airfields and claimed 0-2 planes and 0-1 control tower. A pair of 380th fliers, Maj. McCall and Lt. McKinney, also strafed and claimed 0-6 minesweepers.

(3-0-2 air)

(0-2 ground)

Sqn		Claims
380th:	Lt. T.J. Tilson	(2)FW-190 dest(air)
381st:	Lt. W.A. Webb	FW-190 dest(air)
	Lt. C.H. Smith	FW-190 dam(air)
		Me-109 dam(grd)
		He-111 dam(grd)
	T/Sgt. W.H. Yochim	FW-190 dam(air)

May 20

(#57) Maj. Irvin led 54 P-51s (Lts. Davis, 381st, and Thompson, 382nd, aborted) up at 1012 for an escort mission. Landfall was at 1045 near Le Treport with R/V coming near Wasigny at 1115. After an uneventful escort the pilots crossed out near Cayeaux at 1205 and landed by 1225.

May 21

(#58) 18 P-51s of the 382nd flew a withdrawal support from 1604 to 1805. Landfall came at 1712 over the Somme Estuary and the B-26's were met near Abbeville at 1718. The formations crossed out near St. Quentin at 1720 and after nearing the English coast, the 382nd was informed more bombers were coming out. The squadron turned around, flew back in, saw nothing, then headed for home.

May 23
(#59) With LtCol. Tipton up front, 52 aircraft flew an escort from 0741 to 1055. Except for three aborts (380th-1 381st-2, Lts. Lucas and Stuart), the pilots crossed in at 0820 over Fecamp and made R/V at 0840 west of Tours. The bombers were left at 0955 and afterwards the 381st strafed, claiming 20-0 locos, 20-0 railcars, 8-0 vehicles, and 0-5 flak towers. Landfall-out then followed at 1010 south of Le Havre.

(#60) Maj. Culberson led 12 P-51s of the 381st on a sweep from 1600 to 1830. The planes crossed in at 1633, swept the Mezieres-Liege-Namur-Stavelot area, then headed out at 1805. The lack of enemy resistance was evidently getting to the pilots, as according to the group diary, "We certainly aren't getting many Jerries. But, then, we aren't seeing many."

May 24
(#61) Maj. Irvin led 52 planes on a planned escort from 1004 to 1510. Four 380th pilots aborted and the rest made landfall at 1108 north of Ijmuiden. The Group arrived at the R/V area late and swept the bomber track. The 380th and 382nd then headed out while the 381st strafed from Berlin to Holland (one 382nd flight also strafed an airfield north of Meppel without claims). Claims ran to 22-3 locos, 1-0 truck, 0-5 flak towers, and 0-1 factory with the following pilots scoring: 6-0 locos by Lt. Davis, 4-0 locos by Lt. Freyermuth, 3-0 locos by Lt. Johnson, 3-0 locos and 0-3 flak towers by Lt. Stuart, 2-0 locos by Capt. Dalglish, 1-3 locos by Lt. Recagno, 1-0 loco each by Lts. Gervan and Gallagher, and 1-0 loco, 0-2 flak towers, and 1-0 truck by Lt. Carter. The cost was four pilots lost, one wounded, and two more who made forced-landings. Lt. Richard P. Lucas was hit by flak and bailed out near Ludwigshafen, Lt. Charles H. Smith took a flak hit and bellied-in, and Lt. William R. Schmidt and Lt. Robert E. Kennedy collided while strafing Nordhorn Airfield. Lt. William A. Webb was hit in the legs, stomach, throat, and hands, but managed to make it to Chipping Ongar, while at Staplehurst, both Capt. Dalglish and Lt. Johnson made one-wheel landings due to flak damage.
(4 lost)

May 25
(#62) LtCol. Tipton led 44 aircraft on an escort from 0708 to 1153. Lts. H. Scott and Ringgenberg (381st) aborted and the remainder crossed in at 0745 near Dunkirk. R/V was at 0812 near Namur and the bombers were later left at 1015 over Paris. Several 380th pilots strafed on the way home, with Lts. Haynes, McEachron, Hill, and Steiner claiming 0-2 locos near St. Florentin.

May 26
(#63) Maj. McWherter led 18 P-51s of the 382nd on an escort from 1640 to 1802. The pilots crossed in at 1712 over the Somme Estuary, took some B-26's to the Abbeville area and out, making landfall-out at 1720 near St. Quentin.

May 27
(#64) LtCol. Tipton led 49 planes (Lt. Johnson, 381st, later aborted) on an escort from 1101 to 1550. Landfall was at 1140 near Cayeaux with R/V at 1225 southwest of Troyes. The bombers were taken to Neuenkirchen without problem and landfall-out came at 1422 near Furness.

May 28
(#65) Maj. McWherter led 52 P-51s on an escort from 1149 to 1700. Lts. Gallagher and Ringgenberg (381st) aborted and the rest crossed in at 1255 near Ijmuiden. R/V was then made near Celle at 1336. Four FW-190's hit the 380th west of Gardelegen and shot down Lt. Feodor Clemovitz. The rest of the Group became involved with these planes and many others and in fights ranging from Gardelegen to Wittenburg claimed 12 kills. In addition, two more pilots were lost: Lt. Curry P. Wilson (382nd) was last seen chasing a Me-109 and Lt. Anthony Ladas (382nd) collided with a 78th Fighter Group P-47 near Gardelegen. Heading out, a 382nd flight strafed a field near Frankfurt and shot up a dozen planes. The bombers were later left at 1600 near Stavelot and the Mustangs crossed out at 1635 near Dunkirk.
(12-4-5 air)
(5-7 ground)
(3 lost)

Sqn		Claims
380th:	Lt. E.E. Vance	(2)Me-109 dest(air)
	Lt. G.T. McEachron	Me-109 dest(air)
		Me-109 prob(air)
		Me-410 dam(air)

	Lt. J.E. Hill	FW-190 dest(air)
		FW-190 dam(air)
		Me-410 dam(air)
	Lt. G.C. Clough	Me-410 dest(air)
	Lt. M.A. Kammerlohr	Me-109 dest(air)
		Me-410 dam(air)
	Lt. D.W. Ray	FW-190 dest(air)
	Lt. W.H. Steiner	FW-190 dest(air)
	Lt. B.W. Turner	FW-190 dest(air)
	Lt. B.R. Williams	FW-190 dest(air)
	Lt. H.B. Messer	(.5)Ju-88 prob(air)
	Lt. R.J. Tyler	(.5)Ju-88 prob(air)
381st:	Lt. H.D. Knuppel	FW-190 prob(air)
	Lt. V.T. Johnson	FW-190 dam(air)
382nd:	Maj. R.C. McWherter	Me-109 dest(air)
	Lt. J. Robertson	Me-109 dest(air)
	Lt. J. Jabara	FW-190 prob(air)
	Lt. J.H. Clark	(3)Ju-88 dest(grd)
		He-111 dest(grd)
		He-111 dam(grd)
	Lt. J.R. Brown	He-111 dest(grd)
		(3)u/i a/c dam(grd)
		Ju-52 dam(grd)
	Lt. R.E. Proctor	FW-190 dam(grd)
		Trainer dam(grd)

May 29

(#66) Col. Tipton led 49 planes on an escort from 1022 to 1504. Ten pilots aborted (380th-3 381st-4, Maj. Culberson, Lts. H. Scott, Williams, and T/Sgt. Yochim, 382nd-3) and the rest crossed in at 1128 near Egmond. R/V was made south of Leipzig at 1300 and the bombers were taken to landfall-out near Nieuport at 1445.

May 29

(#67) Maj. McWherter led 14 P-51s of the 382nd on an escort from 1726 to 1920. R/V with some B-26's was at 1745 and the Mustangs later broke and crossed out at 1837 near Schouwen.

May 30

(#68) Col. Tipton led 35 P-51s (Lt. Warner, 382nd, later aborted) of the 380th and 382nd on an escort from 0859 to 1302. The 381st was scheduled to go along but it was discovered that the squadron had no more drop tanks at Staplehurst! They did, however, put up four pilots as relays: Lts. Reinhart, Kemmerer, and Pate and F/O Scott. The planes crossed in at 1003 near

Egmond and at the R/V point, near Dessau, the 382nd was bounced by enemy planes. While claiming 5 kills, Lt. Dale H. Rook was last seen chasing a FW-190 northwest of Dessau and he crashed near Schweintz. Near Burg, the 380th hit eight Me-109's and downed 3 without loss. Heading out, a few 382nd pilots strafed Quackenbruck Airfield and the surrounding area, claiming 0-1 tug and 0-1 crane (both by Lt. Santarlasci), while Lt. Ray of the 380th destroyed a loco west of Arnhem. Lt. Carroll A. Stearns (382nd) was hit by light flak and bellied-in 20 miles south of the Zuider Zee and eventually returned to the Allies control in March of 1945. The 380th then broke at 1200 over Steinhuder Lake and crossed out at 1233 near Egmond. The 382nd broke at 1250 over the Zuider Zee and made landfall-out near Ijmuiden at 1256.

(8-0-2 air)

(2 lost)

Sqn		*Claims*
HdQts:	Col. J.B. Tipton	Me-410 dest(air)
380th:	Maj. M. Cloke	Me-109 dest(air)
		Me-109 dam(air)
	Capt. A.J. Melancon	Me-109 dest(air)
	Lt. J.E. Hill	Me-109 dest(air)
	Lt. E.E. Vance	Me-109 dam(air)
382nd:	Lt. M.A. Thompson	(2)Me-410 dest(air)
	Capt. L.D. Morrison	FW-190 dest(air)
	Lt. J.H. Santarlasci	Me-410 dest(air)

May 31

(#69) Col. Tipton led 50 P-51s on a withdrawal support from 0927 to 1330. Four pilots turned back (380th-2 381st-1, F/O· G. Scott; 382nd-1, Lt. Pavelich) and the remainder made landfall at 1005 near Dunkirk. After much searching the bombers were located southeast of Brussels with R/V at 1215. All planes crossed out with the heavies at 1231 south of Walcheren without incident.

Another interesting quote came on this date in the group diary, "As late as the 31st of May we were still catching that bitter pill of 'pants-acher' escort missions to Berlin and beyond. When other groups were going out and knocking the hell out of the Luftwaffe and the Jerry rail system, we were still playing nursemaid to a bunch of heavies."

June 2

(#70) Maj. McCall led 45 planes on a dive-bombing effort from 1726 to 1843. Lt. Schmidt (382nd) aborted and the rest crossed in at 1805 near St. Valery. While the 381st gave cover, the other squadrons scored hits on the approaches to one bridge and in the middle of a second.

June 4

(#71) Maj. McCall led 18 P-51s of the 380th on an escort from 1426 to 1525. Except for one abort, the planes crossed in at 1450 north of Calais. The pilots then patrolled the Marck area as the B-26's attacked their targets then crossed out at 1510 near Sangathe.

(#72) 17 planes of the 382nd flew an escort from 1450 to 1545. The pilots made landfall at 1509 near Gravelines and made R/V with the B-26's at 1516. After escort was broken the P-51s crossed out near Calais at 1518.

(#73) Maj. Culberson led 18 planes of the 381st on an escort from 1542 to 1650. R/V was made over the Channel at 1607 with landfall near Ault at 1610. After the B-26's were finished all planes crossed out south of Cayeaux at 1615 and escort was broken at 1631 near Friston.

June 6

(#74) Col. Tipton led 50 aircraft up at 2103 for a C-47 escort to the invasion area. Lts. Kunz and Reeves (382nd) aborted and the rest R/V'd at 2205 south of Portland Bill. The planes crossed in at 2300 southwest of Caen and the C-47's were taken to St. Mere Eglise. Escort was later broken at 2305 southeast of Pointe Barfleur. One FW-190 was seen north of St. Mere Eglise but no contact was made. Everyone then headed home and landed at 0034 on June 7.

June 7

(#75) Maj. Irvin led 45 planes on a transport escort from 0556 to 0830. The pilots reached the R/V area at 0635 but no other aircraft were seen. Finally at 0730 some C-47's were picked up north of Pointe Barfleur and taken to Portland Bill, being left at 0807.

(#76) Col. Tipton led 48 planes on a dive-bombing mission from 1918 to 2145. Three P-51's aborted and the rest made landfall at 2015 west of Grandcamp. Attacking targets in the Dieppe-Rennes area, one bridge was damaged northwest of Covin, one was destroyed and a second damaged east of Airel, and other claims were 1-0 loco and 1-0 switch-house. Everyone later crossed out at 2040 near St. Pierre du Mont.

June 8

(#77) Maj. Irvin led 49 planes on a sweep from 1300 to 1547. The Group crossed in at 1326 near Dieppe and swept the Le Mans-St. Valery area. The ships later crossed out at 1512 near St. Valery.

June 10

(#78) Lt. Williams led 4 P-51s of the 380th on a transport escort from 1525 to 1845. The planes made R/V with medical C-47's at 1600 over Anvil Point, later crossed in at St. Mere Eglise at 1626, then circled as the transports were loaded on an airfield near Asnelles-Sur-Mer. Afterwards, the C-47's were taken back to England.

(#79) Maj. Culberson led 16 P-51s of the 381st on a C-47 escort from 1619 to 1850. The pilots made R/V with six glider-towing C-47's at 1658 near St. Albans Head and landfall came at 1740 northeast of St. Mere Eglise. The planes were then escorted back across the Channel and left at 1820 near St. Albans Head.

June 11

(#80) Maj. McCall led 16 planes of the 380th on a dive-bombing mission from 0900 to 1132. One pilot aborted and the rest made landfall at 0945 near Grandcamp. Pilots then dive-bombed in the Vire-Caumont-St. Lô area, scoring hits on a bridge at St. Suzanne Sur Vire and on a repair shop at Garfalout. Lt. Edwin E. Vance was hit by flak and crashed near Carentan, while Lt. William W. Huff's Mustang was also damaged. He managed to reach the English coast before bailing out and being picked up by ASR. The rest of the squadron crossed out at 1045 near Grandcamp. Blue Flight also chased a FW-190 west of St. Lô but it escaped in the clouds.

(2 lost-1 rescued)

(#81) Maj. Cloke led 45 planes on a planned dive-bombing mission from 1609 to 1655. Due to weather conditions the planes were recalled while nearing the Continent.

June 12

(#82) Maj. Cloke led 16 P-51s of the 380th on a C-47 escort from 0634 to 0922. R/V was made at 0728 and the planes crossed in at 0800 near Bel de Cruttes. The pilots circled St. Mere Eglise while the transports dropped supplies then escorted them back out, making landfall at 0805 near Hau du Nord. The C-47's were later left at 0845 near St. Albans Head.

(#83) Maj. Culberson led 16 P-51s of the 381st on a B-26 support from 0733 to 1010. The pilots made R/V at 0810 over Beachy Head and crossed in at 0827 near St. Valery. After bombing in the Conflans area, all planes crossed out at 0935 near St. Valery and the bombers were left at 0955 near Beachy Head.

(#84) Four P-51s of the 382nd flew an escort for a C-53 from 0845 to 1130. The pilots made R/V at 0920 over Selsey Bill, crossed in at 1000 near St. Pierre du Mont then circled while the C-53 landed. The transport took off again at 1030 and the planes crossed out at 1034 over St. Pierre du Mont. Escort was terminated at 1112 near Selsey Bill.

(#85) Four P-51s of the 382nd flew a transport escort from 0900 to 1300. The Mustangs landed at Middle Wallop at 0935 and took off with the C-47 at 1015, all planes making landfall at 1120 near Raz de la Percee. The transport landed at 1122 and the Mustangs circled while it was unloaded. The C-47 then took-off and was escorted across the Channel and left at the English coast.

(#86) Lt. Nicholas led 4 P-51s of the 380th on a withdrawal support from 1702 to 1913. The pilots reached the assigned area near Granville, but the B-17 they were looking for was never found. While circling, Lt. Maurice W. Hollowell was hit by flak north of Bayeaux and his aircraft started to smoke. He bailed out southwest of Douvres at 1,500 feet but his chute failed.

(1 lost)

June 13

(#87) Lt. Boland led 33 P-51s of the 381st and 382nd on an escort from 0620 to 0831. The planes crossed in at 0700 near Fecamp and R/V'd with the B-26's at 0705. The bombers attacked targets in the Domfront area and on the way out, Capt. Brown (382nd) strafed a boat on the Seine causing some damage. The pilots then crossed out at 0744 north of Caen.

(#88) Maj. Irvin led 50 Mustangs on a dive-bombing mission from 2023 to 2250. Landfall was at 2120 near Grandcamp and the pilots attacked targets in the Avranches-Vire-Lessay area. A marshalling yard at La Repas was hit, one bridge near Mortain was damaged, and four other bridges northwest of Avranches were also damaged. Other targets were hit northwest of Cuves for claims of 1-0 car and 15-10 railcars. Landfall was then made at 2155 in the Grandcamp area.

June 14

(#89) 50 P-51s flew a dive-bombing mission in the Torigny-Vire area from 1102 to 1325. The planes crossed in at 1138 near Fecamp and reached the area at 1206. Their main target, a railway gun, was barely seen, so bombs were dropped in the area and one squadron hit a marshalling yard north of Vire, claiming 0-4 buildings. After reassembling, the pilots crossed out at 1224 near Fecamp.

(#90) With Maj. Cloke leading, 48 P-51s flew a dive-bombing mission in the Crez-en-Bonere/Laval area from 1739 to 2015. The pilots made landfall at 1815 near La Havre and proceeded to attack targets. The 380th scored hits on tracks northeast of La Cosse le Viven and southeast of Laval, plus Capt. Melancon and Lt. Steiner claimed 1-0 truck by strafing near Bleu Sur Mer. The 381st hit tracks north of Bouers-Bouesey and Lt. Munder claimed 0-1 truck and trailer north of Sable. The 382nd scored hits on a rail junction which wiped out the tracks, and two P-51's strafed a marshalling yard northeast of Laval causing some damage to the over 200 railcars there. Two Mustangs were also downed, both apparently caused by damage from bomb blasts. Lt. Arthur M. Mimler (381st) and Lt. James E. Hill (380th) both went down southeast of Laval and were captured. The rest crossed out at 1930 north of Fecamp.

(2 lost)

June 15

(#91) Col. Tipton led 49 planes on a dive-bombing mission to the Laval area from 0620 to 0810. Lt. Thoresz (381st) aborted and the rest crossed in at 0645 near Fecamp and then attacked marshalling yards southwest of Sable and northeast of Laval. Claims amounted to 0-20 railcars, 1-0 truck, 1-3 bridges, 0-1 rail station. Two FW-190's were spotted by a pair of 380th pilots west of Laval and after jettisoning their bombs, the duo downed both Focke Wulfs.

(2-0-0 air)

Sqn		Claims
380th:	Lt. W.M. Haynes	FW-190 dest(air)
	Lt. T.J. Tilson	FW-190 dest(air)

(#92) Maj. McWherter led 49 planes on a dive-bombing mission to the Granville-Coutances area from 1842 to 2100. The Mustangs crossed in at 1930 near St. Mere Eglise and then split-up: the 380th hit the marshalling yard at Hymouville tearing up tracks and also scored hits on buildings in a yard northeast of Laval. The 381st attacked a marshalling yard at Granville which saw a number of hits start fires, and the 382nd hits the yards at Orval and Folligny which tore up tracks. Claims came to 1-7 buildings while one P-51 was lost. Lt. Edward J. Vesely (381st) was hit by flak near Granville and bailed out west of St. Lô. He evaded capture and returned to Allied lines in August. The rest of the Group later crossed out at 2010 east of St. Mere Eglise.

(1 lost)

June 17

(#93) Col. Tipton led 16 aircraft of the 382nd on a patrol in the St. Lô area from 0704 to 1005. The planes made landfall at 1813 near the Carentan Estuary and bombed in the Folligny and Camisy areas, claiming 0-2 railcars. Heading out, Lt. Donald E. Williams was forced to crash-land at Emergency Landing Ground #4 but he was uninjured. The rest of the Mustangs crossed out over Carentan at 1915.

(#94) Capt. Dalglish led 18 P-51s of the 381st on a dive-bombing show from 0825 to 1040. The pilots crossed in at 0916 near Cape Levy (except Lt. Williams who had aborted) and hit targets south of St. Lô and near Conde-Sur-Vire. Claims amounted to 2-0 locos, 2-1 railcars, and 0-1 bridge, but three pilots were lost: Lt. Edward W. Kemmerer was hit by ground fire and bailed out near Cerisy-la-Salle; Lt. Virgil T. Johnson was lost in the Tessy area; and T/Sgt. Walter H. Yochim simply disappeared. The rest of the planes crossed out at 0940 near Maissy.

(3 lost)

(#95) Maj. McCall led 16 aircraft of the 380th on an Armed Recon in the St. Jean de Daye area from 0903 to 1211. The planes made landfall at 1050 near Grandcamp and later crossed out over the same area at 1130. A convoy was bombed with good results while more trucks were attacked near a woods with unknown results. Lt. Herbert F. Lyman was hit by flak on the flight and crashed southeast of Savigny.

(1 lost)

(#96) Capt. Morrison led 11 P-51s of the 382nd on an Armed Recon in the Lessay-Marigny area from 1225 to 1510. The planes made landfall at 1307 near the Carentan Estuary and then attacked targets south of Marigny, Perey, and southeast of Canisy, claiming 1-0 loco and 2-0 staff cars. One flight also sighted 4 FW-190's near Folligny and shot down one. The squadron later crossed out at 1420 over the Carentan Estuary

except for Lt. Kozaczka, who landed on an emergency strip with a damaged aileron.

(1-0-0 air)

Sqn		Claims
382nd:	Lt. J.W. Schmidt	FW-190 dest(air)

(#97) Capt. Dalglish led 14 P-51s of the 381st on a dive-bombing mission in the Coutances area from 1437 to 1654. The pilots crossed in at 1530 near Granville and upon reaching their assigned area, the truck convoy could not be found. They later saw 40 more trucks and bombed them with unknown results. The planes then turned for home with landfall-out at 1550 near Lessay.

(#98) Maj. McCall led 15 planes of the 380th on an Armed Recon in the St. Jean de Daye area from 1601 to 1803. They made landfall at 1645 near Grandcamp then strafed a convoy near Periere, claiming 1-6 trucks. Everyone then crossed out at 1720 near Grandcamp.

(#99) Capt. Morrison led 12 planes of the 382nd on an Armed Recon in the St. Lô area from 1728 to 2005. Landfall was at 1813 over the Carentan Estuary and after an uneventful patrol, the pilots headed out over the same area at 1915. The only known claims were for 2-0 trucks, both destroyed by Lt. Bingham, while a number of hits were registered on an intersection and woods where a dispersal area was thought to be.

(#100) Capt. Dalglish led 16 P-51s of the 381st on an Armed Recon in the St. Lô area from 1948 to 2132. Landfall-in was at 2030 and the pilots bombed a wooded area northeast of St. Lô plus strafed some huts in the same area. Landfall-out then came at 2040.

(#101) Maj. McCall led 14 planes of the 380th on an Armed Recon in the St. Lô area from 2030 to 2215. The Mustangs crossed in at 2110 near Grandcamp then strafed a convoy in the St. Sampson/Conde-Sur-Vire area, claiming 1-12 trucks. The pilots later crossed out at 2135 near Grandcamp.

June 18

(#102) Maj. McWherter led 14 P-51s of the 382nd on an Armed Recon in the Cherbourg area from 0555 to 0812. Two pilots (Lts. Clark and Bortle) aborted and the rest made landfall at 0638 near Les Grieves. Bombs were dropped on coastal gun positions with poor results, plus 1-0 truck was claimed by strafing. Everyone later crossed out at 0715 near Cape de Carteret.

(#103) Maj. Culberson led 16 P-51s of the 381st on an Armed Recon in the Valognes area from 0730 to 0935. The planes made landfall at 0810 near Quineville, then dive-bombed in the Valognes area, claiming 0-1 railcar and 0-1 building. Afterwards the pilots crossed out at 0847 near Quineville.

(#104) Capt. DeLong led 16 Mustangs of the 380th on an Armed Recon in the Bricquebec area from 0852 to 1050. The fighters made landfall at 0938 near St. Vaast then hit targets southwest of Bricquebec, claiming 2-0 trucks and 4-0 horse-drawn carts. The planes later crossed out at 1002 near Ravenville.

(#105) 11 P-51s of the 382nd flew an Armed Recon in the Cherbourg area from 1022 to 1237. The planes crossed in at 1101 near St. Vaast then attacked targets west of Valognes, claiming 0-6 railcars and 0-1 radio tower. Landfall-out then followed at 1135 near St. Vaast.

(#106) Maj. Culberson led 14 P-51s of the 381st on an Armed Recon in the Cherbourg area from 1154 to 1450. Lt. Ringgenberg aborted and the rest crossed in at 1232 near Quineville and then strafed near Bricquebec, claiming 1-2 tanks, 9-5 trucks, and 3-0 motorcycles. In addition, a wooded area was dive-bombed with unknown results. The pilots then made landfall-out at 1318 near Quineville.

(#107) Maj. McCall led 15 planes of the 380th on an Armed Recon from 1320 to 1515. Crossing in at 1402 near St. Pierre du Mont, gun positions near Bois-de-Norest were bombed with poor results. The pilots then crossed out at 1435 near St. Vaast.

(#108) Maj. McWherter led 12 planes of the 382nd on an Armed Recon in the Cherbourg area from 1457 to 1700. The pilots crossed in at 1532 near St. Martin and bombed south of Cherbourg and near Grosville with unknown results before crossing out near St. Martin at 1611. Lt. Brink took a flak hit and after returning to England his engine caught fire. He bailed out near Turnbridge Wells and returned to the group a couple days later.

(#109) Maj. Culberson led 16 planes of the 381st on an Armed Recon in the Bricquebec area from 1620 to 1845. The pilots crossed in at 1703 then attacked a number of targets. Anti-aircraft positions and barracks were dive-bombed at Les Pleusz

but no hits were observed; some gun emplacements at Couville were damaged by bombs, and strafing netted 0-1 tank, 1-0 wagon, 0-1 gun position, and 0-1 barracks. The ships later crossed out at 1804 near Quineville.

(#110) Capt. DeLong led 15 planes of the 380th on an Armed Recon in the Valognes-Bricquebec area from 1750 to 1945. The P-51s crossed in at 1830 near St. Vaast and hit targets near Coreville, Grosville, and Negrevil, claiming 0-1 bridge and 5-0 trucks. The pilots later crossed out at 1808 near Quineville.

(#111) Capt. Morrison led 14 planes of the 382nd on an Armed Recon in the Cherbourg area from 1921 to 2130. Crossing in at 2005 near St. Vaast, targets were hit northwest of Hordinvast, southwest of Cherbourg, and near Bricquebec. Claims amounted to 1-0 radio tower, 1-0 ammo dump, and 1-0 bridge with the planes crossing out at 2035 near St. Vaast.

It was during this time that the Germans sent a number of V-1's over and around Staplehurst. The group diary for the 18th stated, "Just at midnight the field was attacked by German rocket planes, ack-ack, and a tremendous case of jitters. A red alert was given and at the same time the first rocket plane flew over the field at tree-top level, with streams of tracers following it as it buzzed. Then came our first battle order over the speaker system, 'Look out for rockets, and do what you think best!'. The officers and enlisted men did just that, 'best' varying from dressing themselves with gun, helmet, and gas mask, to merely staying in the sack. Later a warning came that paratroopers had landed within fifteen miles. The reaction to this varied from going in an orderly manner to pre-determined posts, to running around in circles howling 'Achtung, Luftwaffe!'. This continued until about 9 a.m. Fortunately, no one was hurt and several of the 'Buck Rogers Specials' were shot down."

June 19

(#112) Capt. Dalglish led 16 P-51s of the 381st on an Armed Recon from 0716 to 0920. The planes crossed in at 0800 near Quittenhow and due to heavy cloud cover, turned for home. Lt. James W. White was last seen heading out and failed to return. The rest of the squadron made landfall at 0815 near St. Marcoufat.

(1 lost)

(#113) Maj. McCall led 41 Mustangs on a dive-bombing mission from 2014 to 2140. Two 380th pilots aborted and the rest made landfall near Calais at 2040. Targets were hit near Calais,

Lambus En Ponthieu, and Forette Claimoraus, with claims of 0-2 barges, 2-0 buildings, 4-0 houses, 0-2 radio towers, and 0-1 V-1 ramp. Lt. Ernest L. Nicholas (380th) was hit by flak over Calais and crashed 10 miles off Cape Gris Nez. The rest of the P-51s crossed out at 2100 near Boulogne.

(1 lost)

During the evening of the 19th, Capt. Dalglish and Lts. Davis, Stuart, and Henry (381st) were sent up to intercept some V-1's. Sighting a rocket near Hastings, Dalglish brought it down in the Penhurst area. His combat report follows, "Was vectored onto rocket in Hastings area by SNACKBAR. When I first saw him, I was at 6000 feet and the rocket at 1500. I dove past two Spitfires and a Mustang which were firing at him and I closed on him, indicating about 450 MPH. He was indicating about 400 MPH. Started firing from about 1000 yards but did not register hits until about 400 yards. Scored hits at both wingroots and he chandelled to the right and went down in a descending turn, finally crashing in a wooded area near Penhurst. This occurred about 2205."

June 20

(#114) Col. Tipton led 39 P-51s on a penetration-target-withdrawal support from 0629 to 1127. Five planes aborted (380th-1 381st-1, Lt. Boland, 382nd-3) and the rest made landfall at 0745 near Egmond. R/V with the 8th Air Force bombers followed at 0826 in the Luchow area. North of Dessau, the 380th engaged 40-plus Germans and downed 6 while Lt. Bruce W. Turner was lost near Wittenburg. Heading out, Tipton strafed an airfield in the Ulzen area and burned one plane, while Lts. Gervan and Jacobson (381st) strafed on the route out and claimed 3-1 locos. Landfall then came at 1035 near Terschelling and the bombers were left shortly after.

(6-0-8 air)
(1-0 ground)
(1 lost)

Sqn		Claims
HdQts:	Col. J.B. Tipton	Do-217 dest(grd)
380th:	Lt. W.H. Steiner	(2)Me-109 dest(air)
	Capt. R.C. Fletcher	Me-109 dest(air)
		Ju-88 dam(air)
	Lt. T.S.L. McClung	Me-109 dest(air)
	Lt. G.T. McEachron	Me-410 dest(air)
		(2)Me-109 dam(air)
	Lt. B.R. Williams	Me-109 dest(air)
	Lt. L.F. Reetzke	FW-190 dam(air)
		(3)Me-410 dam(air)
		FW-190 dam(air)

(#115) LtCol. Irvin led 36 planes up at 2053 for an Armed Recon in the Bonniers area. Irvin aborted on the way across and Lt. Tilson then took the lead. The P-51's crossed in at 2129 near Le Treport and proceeded to Onles/Treport, where they split and hit targets near Crespteres, Villiers, St. Andre de L'Eure, and Houdon. Claims amounted to 0-2 bridges, 8-7 railcars, 4-8 machine gun nests, 1-0 flak tower, and 1-1 buildings. Everyone then crossed out at 2220 near Le Treport and the last ship was down by 2318.

June 21

(#116) Col. Tipton led 44 P-51s on a penetration-target-withdrawal support from 0742 to 1326. Eight pilots aborted (380th-3 381st-1, Lt. Pate, 382nd-4) and the rest crossed in at 0854 north of Ijmuiden. Lt. Willard V. Hamilton (382nd) was one of the aborts (due to a coolant leak) and he bailed out over the North Sea to be captured. R/V was made at 1002 near Dummer Lake and the bombers were taken to Berlin. Near Potsdam, a straggling B-24 was picked up by a 381st flight, but upon nearing it, the bomber veered away. Heavy flak then burst around the P-51s followed by two Me-109's attempting a bounce. One Messerschmitt was shot down and the second flew off. The Group then swept the bomber track back out and made landfall at 1229 near Ijmuiden.

(1-0-0 air)
(1 lost)

Sqn		Claims
381st:	Lt. P.H. Henry	Me-109 dest(air)

(#117) LtCol. Irvin led 14 planes on a dive-bombing mission from 1820 to 2020. Landfall came at 1848 near Tecqueville and a bridge near Epernon was then attacked. Two direct hits were made on the bridge with a number of other hits on the embankment. While heading home, 15 FW-190's passed over one 381st flight and these were in turn hit by another flight with 2 being destroyed.

(2-0-0 air)

Sqn		Claims
381st:	Lt. P.W. Wood	(2)FW-190 dest(air)

At Staplehurst, the first elements of the group began to make the move for France. The air echelon went to the marshaling area at Winchester, then traveled in trucks to Southampton on the 24th. They boarded a Liberty Ship the same day and sailed in the evening. The men were unloaded on Utah Beach on June 25, then were sent to a P-47 strip northeast of Monteburg on the 26th. By June 30, the men were at Maupertus and they started to get the facilities ready for the rest of the group.

June 22

(#118) LtCol. Irvin led 43 planes on a dive-bombing mission from 1208 to 1345. The pilots made landfall at 1301 near Biville then hit targets in the La Roche-Martinvast area. Claims were made for 1-2 bridges, 0-1 building, and 0-2 hangars before landfall-out at 1306 near Quineville.

(#119) Col. Tipton led 44 P-51s on a dive-bombing mission from 1959 to 2330. Four planes aborted (380th-1 381st-1, Lt. Munder, 382nd-2) and the rest made landfall at 2050 near Grandcamp. Targets were attacked in the La Rochelle-Belleville area with claims of 0-2 bridges. Everyone then crossed out at 2220 near Grandcamp.

June 23

(#120) Capt. Dalglish led 16 P-51s of the 381st on an Armed Recon in the Torigny-Gouver-Villedon area from 0745 to 1020. The planes crossed in at 0832 near Grandcamp and claims amounted to 4-2 trucks, 1-0 half-track, 1-0 motorcycle, 0-30 railcars, and 0-4 gas tanks. Everyone later crossed out at 0935 near Grandcamp.

(#121) Capt. Morrison led 16 P-51s of the 382nd on a sweep. Taking off at 0912, the mission was recalled due to weather at 0925.

(#122) Maj. McWherter led 16 P-51s of the 382nd on an Armed Recon southwest of Cherbourg from 1643 to 1950. One Mustang aborted and the rest made landfall at 1726 near Grandcamp. Strafing netted 0-20 trucks and 5-0 tanks, then at 1822, near Mortain, 10 Me-109's were encountered. 4 were destroyed without loss and the pilots then crossed out at 1835 near St. Homorine.

(4-0-2 air)

Sqn		Claims
382nd:	Maj. R.C. McWherter	(2)Me-109 dest(air)

Lt. J.N. Brink	Me-109 dest(air)
Lt. J.R. Stricker	Me-109 dest(air)
Lt. R.E. Proctor	Me-109 dam(air)
Lt. L.E. Webster	Me-109 dam(air)

(#123) Maj. McCall led 16 P-51s of the 380th on an Armed Recon in the Torigny-Gourets area from 1800 to 2000. The pilots made landfall at 1840 near Torigny and claimed 30-4 trucks, 3-0 tanks, and 1-0 bridge in the Gourets-Torigny area. The ships later crossed out at 1925 near Grandcamp.

(#124) Maj. Culberson led 16 P-51s of the 381st on an Armed Recon to Mortain from 1930 to 2208. The fighters made landfall at 2014 near Grandcamp (minus Lt. Shea who aborted) and then hit targets near Percy, Margueray, Villedieu, and Traebebrey, claiming 8-0 trucks, 2-0 motorcycles, 1-0 auto, 0-2 tanks, 1-0 bridge, 2-5 buildings, and 4-0 gas tanks. The squadron later crossed out at 2115 near Grandcamp.

June 24

(#125) Maj. McCall led 48 planes on a dive-bombing mission in the Chartres area from 0707 to 0902. One pilot aborted and the rest made landfall at 0744 near Fecamp. Claims were made for 0-6 railcars and 0-4 bridges (one at Chartresky by the 380th, one at Cloyes by the 381st, and two near Beaugency by the 382nd). Capt. Martin L. DeLong (380th) was hit by flak from an airfield near Dreux and bailed out over the Channel where he was picked up by ASR. The rest of the Group crossed out near Fecamp at 0840.

(1 lost)

(#126) Maj. Cloke led 12 P-51s (from all three squadrons) on a dive-bombing mission to Le Touzey from 1218 to 1432. The pilots crossed in at 1310 near St. Mere Eglise and during their attacks claimed 2-0 trucks, 0-1 bridge, and 0-4 houses. The Mustangs later crossed out near St. Mere Eglise at 1340.

(#127) 16 P-51s of the 382nd flew an Armed Recon in the Vire area from 1230 to 1540. Crossing in at 1316 over the Carentan Estuary, pilots claimed 0-1 bridge and 1-0 tank north of Flers. On flight also strafed a bellied-in RAF Typhoon east of Thury-Marcourt; they registered a number of hits but the fighter failed to burn. Twelve of the planes crossed out at 1414 near the Carentan Estuary while one flight made landfall near Grandcamp at 1452.

(#128) Maj. Culberson led 19 P-51s of the 381st on a dive-bombing mission to the Lessay-Periers area from 1315 to 1516. The planes made landfall at 1402 near Vierville and they later crossed out in the same area at 1438. The only claim was for 1-0 bridge, hit near Lessay.

(#129) LtCol. Irvin led 40 P-51s on a dive-bombing effort in the Chartres-Cloyes-Flers-Loire area from 1815 to 2018. Landfall came at 1901 near Fecamp and claims on the mission came to 10-0 railcars, 0-2 bridges, and 0-1 truck. Lt. Paul F. Clark (381st) bailed out northwest of Bonneval after getting caught in a bomb blast and he later returned to Allied control. The remaining pilots crossed out at 2002 near Fecamp.

(1 lost)

June 25

(#130) Maj. McWherter led 13 P-51s of the 382nd on an Armed Recon in the Argentan-Dreux area from 0610 to 0935. One pilot aborted and the rest crossed in at 0654 near Dives Sur Mer. East of Lisieux, a fight was observed between some P-38's and German fighters and the 382nd headed for the battle. Enroute, a dozen more enemy planes were encountered and 4 were shot down against two losses. Lt. Marvin A. Thompson bellied-in near Beauvais and evaded capture, but Lt. Harrie A. Winham was killed.

(4-1-4 air)

(2 lost)

Sqn		Claims
382nd:	Lt. D.L. King	Me-109 dest(air)
		Me-109 prob(air)
		Me-109 dam(air)
	Lt. J.H. Santarlasci	Me-109 dest(air)
		FW-190 dam(air)
	Lt. R.W. Asbury	(.5)FW-190 dest(air)*
		Me-109 dam(air)
	Lt. J. Jabara	(.5)FW-190 dest(air)*
	Lt. M.A. Thompson	(.5)FW-190 dest(air)**
	Lt. H.A. Winham	(.5)FW-190 dest(air)**
	Lt. R.M. Heberlein	Me-109 dam(air)

(#131) Maj. Cloke led 13 P-51s of the 380th on an Armed Recon in the Argentan-Dreux area from 0825 to 1108. The pilots crossed in at 0911 near Haulgate and hit targets in the Bivillers-Tourovre area. Making attacks from 0925 to 1025, claims were 5-3 trucks, 3-0 jeeps, 1-0 tank, 1-0 auto, and 3-0 weapons carriers. Everyone later crossed out at 1045 near Haulgate.

(#132) Lt. Carter led 14 planes of the 381st on an Armed Recon in the Argentan-Dreux area from 1205 to 1445. The ships made landfall at 1300 near Cabourg and the pilots claimed 8-0 railcars, 4-4 trucks, and 2-0 autos. In addition, a highway overpass was destroyed and tracks torn up near St. Martin. The Mustangs later crossed out north of Caen at 1405.

(#133) Capt. Morrison led 10 P-51s of the 382nd on an Armed Recon in the Argentan area from 1304 to 1613. Lt. Pawlak aborted and the rest made landfall at 1351 near Dives Sur Mer. Claims were for 1-1 autos near Verneuil, 0-1 bridge west of Dreux, and a rail junction and railcars damaged plus tracks torn up south of Dreux. The pilots later crossed out at 1525 near Dives Sur Mer.

(#134) Capt. Melancon led 12 P-51s of the 380th on a dive-bombing mission to the Bernay area from 1400 to 1642. One pilot aborted and the rest crossed in at 1448 near Bayeaux. The planes made attacks from 1455 to 1540 and claimed 1-0 truck near La Neuve Lyre and bombed 20 railcars with poor results near Bernay. Lt. Lyle F. Reetzke was hit by flak near Breuteuil and later bailed out near Coulmer. The rest of the 380th crossed at 1600 near Bayeaux.

(1 lost)

Pilots of the 381st were also involved in more V-1 intercepts on this date. Capt. Dalglish was again involved and his report read, "No friendly fighters present so I went into attack from 5000 feet at 400 MPH and got several good bursts in the 'diver', which made columns of flames coming from tail increase. Overshot, but 'diver' was still on course, so I made a second attack which caused 'diver' to spin into the ground and explode about 15 miles south of the Thames. Headed southwest and picked up another 'diver' over Headoorn and went into attack from 4000 feet at 350 MPH. Got several good bursts into 'diver', which caused it to loop twice and then hit the ground and explode about 2230."

June 27

(#135) Maj. McCall led 33 planes on a dive-bombing mission to the Laille-Nantes area from 1508 to 1735. Three pilots aborted and the rest made landfall at 1528 near Montebourg. Claims amounted to 5-30 railcars southwest of Redon, 0-15 trucks near St. Melaine, 1-0 auto north of Nantes, 0-1 radio station southwest of Nantes, and 0-2 bridges, one at Laille and the other southwest of Bouaye. The Mustangs later crossed out at 1700 near Montebourg.

(#136) Col. Tipton led 36 P-51s on an Armed Recon in the Redon-Masseran-Blain area from 1910 to 2211. Crossing in at 2005 near Montebourg (except for Lt. Boland, 381st, who aborted), the ships reached the area at 2022. Claims were made for 2-4 locos and 66-35 railcars, plus rails were torn up east of Redon and near Bain de Bretegne. The pilots later crossed out at 2130 near Montebourg.

During the evening, Capt. Dalglish and Lt Freyermuth (381st) were sent up on a V-1 intercept. According to Freyermuth's report, "I sighted a P-(pilotless) plane about 3 miles east of base at about 2005, closed to within 300 yards, chasing it for approximately five minutes, firing intermittent bursts. P-plane finally swung to right, dove to the ground, and exploded about five miles west of Maidstone."

June 29
(#137) Col. Tipton led 38 planes on an 8th Air Force bomber escort from 0649 to 1159. Lts. Richardson and Pate (381st) aborted and the rest crossed in at 0735 near Schouwen. R/V was accomplished at 0856 near Leipzig and the bombers were later left over the Zuider Zee. Landfall-out then came north of Ijmuiden at 1120. During the flight, a single Me-109 was seen near Giessen and shot down, while Lt. Paul W. Wood (381st) was last seen in the same area.

(1-0-0 air)

(1 lost)

Sqn		Claims
381st:	Lt. P.H. Henry	Me-109 dest(air)

The 381st continued its war against the V-1's, as later in the day, Lt. John Gervan shot one down over the Channel. His report read, "First seen southeast of Folkestone, about mid-Channel, and shot down about 3 to 5 miles from shore, between Folkestone and Dungeness. Altitude 2000 feet; speed approximately 300 MPH; time was approximately 2030; range 150 yards. The rocket was below me and I turned into it out of a right turn, closing into range. Fired about four bursts, saw strikes on the machine, bits of the right wing flew off, then the flames stopped and it veered off on its left wing into the Channel."

Also, Lt. Elmo H. Berglind (381st) returned for a visit to the Group after having evaded capture since his loss on March 18.

June 30
(#138) 36 P-51s flew a dive-bombing mission to the Arveile-Orleans-Chartres area from 0656 to 0943. The planes crossed in at 0740 near Fecamp and reached the area at 0820. Claims amounted to 0-2 locos, 0-46 railcars, 0-2 trucks, 0-1 bridge, and 0-1 building before everyone made landfall-out at 0915 near Fecamp.

(#139) Capt. Fletcher led 36 planes (Lt. Williams and F/O Scott, 381st, later aborted) on a dive-bombing mission to the Beaugency-Cloyes-Arroi-Chateaudun area from 1455 to 1755. The pilots crossed in at 1540 near Fecamp and later left over the same area at 1645. The 380th claimed 0-2 bridges, near Cloyes and Beaugency, and 0-30 railcars at a marshalling yard near Orleans. The 381st claimed 0-1 bridge near Arrou and 0-2 trucks and 0-2 railcars near Courtalain. 382nd pilots claimed 0-1 bridge south of Chateaudun. The 380th spotted a Me-109 near Dreux but made no contact, while another 109 passed through the 381st west of Boullay and likewise avoided contact.

July 1
(#140) Capt. Tilson led 4 P-51s of the 380th on a C-47 escort from 1700 to 1845. R/V was made at 1720 over Selsy Bill and landfall came near St. Pierre du Mont at 1800. The C-47 landed here and the Mustangs then headed home.

On this same day, Maj. Marshall Cloke was sent home on leave and he turned command of the 380th over to Capt. Louis D. Morrison. Taking Morrison's place as Operations Officer of the 382nd was Capt. John R. Brown.

July 4
(#141) Col. Tipton led 35 P-51s on a mission to dive-bomb gun positions in the Coutances area from 0855 to 1130. Three planes aborted and the rest made landfall at 0955 near Hague Forts. Heavy ground fire and bad weather were encountered and five pilots were MIA. Lt. John W. Oyler and Lt. Charles R. Reddig (380th) each bailed out northeast of Coutances after flak hits; Lt. Kenneth W. Doran and Lt. Harold E. Scott (381st) were knocked down by flak south of St. Lô; and Lt. John Gervan (381st) was last seen in the same area. The guns were never seen, so bombs were dropped on flak areas near Coutances with unknown results. Landfall-out later came at 1030 near Hague Forts.

(5 lost)

During the evening the pilots flew their planes to France. New home for the 363rd was Advanced Landing Ground-15, Maupertus, on the Cherbourg Peninsula. Maupertus was an ex-Luftwaffe field and while the facilities were heavily damaged, the men were put to work making the base both usable and livable. The air echelon, which had arrived on June 30, was set-up and missions would begin on July 5.

July 5
(#142) 10 P-51s of the 380th flew an Armed Recon in the Mayenne area from 2010 to 2100. The planes arrived in the area at 2025 and carried out an uneventful mission. 8-9 trucks were seen near Periers but no attacks were made.

(#143) Lt. Gallagher led 10 planes of the 381st on an Armed Recon in the Mayenne area from 2045 to 2200. The mission was uneventful as nothing was seen.

(#144) Capt. Brown led 12 P-51s of the 382nd on an Armed Recon in the St. Lô-Mortain area from 2110 to 2210. The only claim was 1-0 auto by Capt. Brown near Domfront.

July 6
(#145) Capt. DeLong led 8 planes of the 380th on an Assault Area Patrol in the Cherbourg area from 0650 to 0920.

(#146) 8 P-51s of the 382nd flew a B-26 escort to the Vire area from 0805 to 1005. R/V was made at 0835 and the bombers were left near Le Tout at 0930.

(#147) Lt. Recagno led 8 planes of the 381st on an AAP in the Cherbourg area from 0945 to 1150. The only thing seen was a Spitfire being shot down by flak.

(#148) Capt. Williams led 8 P-51s of the 380th on an AAP in the Cherbourg area from 1245 to 1435.

(#149) Lt. Stuart led 8 planes of the 381st on an AAP in the Cherbourg area from 1540 to 1750.

(#150) Capt. McEachron led 8 Mustangs of the 380th on an AAP in the Cherbourg area from 1845 to 2025.

(#151) 8 P-51s of the 382nd flew an AAP in the Cherbourg area from 2000 to 2150.

(#152) F/O Scott led 8 planes of the 381st on an AAP in the Cherbourg area from 2140 to 2245.

On this date, members of the ground echelon began their move to the staging area at Winchester. Sailing from Southampton on the 7th, the men were off-loaded at Omaha Beach on July 8. They then proceeded to Maupertus and arrived on the 9th.

July 7
(#153) Lt. Thoresz led 8 P-51s of the 381st on an AAP in the Cherbourg area from 0610 to 0810.

(#154) 6 planes of the 382nd flew an AAP in the Cherbourg area from 0820 to 1010.

(#155) Capt. Melancon led 8 pilots of the 380th on an AAP in the Cherbourg area from 0949 to 1210. A FW-190 was seen southeast of St. Lô but it escaped in the clouds.

(#156) Capt. Lasko led 8 P-51s of the 381st on an AAP in the Cherbourg area from 1117 to 1303.

(#157) 8 planes of the 382nd flew an AAP in the Cherbourg area from 1420 to 1602.

(#158) Capt. Melancon led 8 P-51s of the 380th on an AAP in the Cherbourg area from 1540 to 1730.

(#159) Lt. Boland led 8 P-51s of the 381st on an AAP in the Cherbourg area from 1720 to 1910.

(#160) 8 pilots of the 382nd flew an AAP in the Cherbourg area from 2015 to 2200. The planes were vectored to a bogie near Vire and it was thought to be a Ju-88. The pilots opened fire before realizing it was an RAF Mosquito; luckily, little damage was inflicted before breaking off.

(#161) Capt. McEachron led 8 planes of the 380th on an AAP in the Cherbourg area from 2145 to 2250.

July 8
(#162) Lt. Wheeler led 8 P-51s of the 381st on an AAP in the Cherbourg area from 0635 to 0845.

(#163) Capt. Williams led 8 planes of the 380th on a P-47 escort from 0700 to 0900. R/V was at 0730 near Laval and the pilots provided top cover as the Thunderbolts made their attacks. The P-51s were vectored several times but only saw B-17's and B-26's.

(#164) 8 P-51s of the 382nd flew an AAP in the Cherbourg area from 0943 to 1117.

(#165) Lt. Munder led 8 Mustangs of the 381st on an AAP in the Cherbourg area from 1550 to 1738.

(#166) Lt. Clough led 8 P-51s of the 380th on a P-47 cover mission from 1620 to 1755. After watching over the 47's near Vire, the pilots strafed near Margueray and Lt. Sample claimed 1-0 truck.

(#167) Lt. Trumbower led 8 planes of the 381st on an AAP in the Cherbourg area from 1840 to 2040.

(#168) Capt. DeLong led 8 Mustangs of the 380th on a P-47 cover from 2110 to 2220. R/V was made at 2130 near Tessy-Sur-Vire and the 47's were later left in the Bayeaux area at 2155.

(#169) Lt. Brink led 8 P-51s of the 382nd on an AAP in the Cherbourg area from 2140 to 2240.

July 9
(#170) 8 P-51s of the 382nd flew an AAP in the Cherbourg area from 0805 to 1015.

(#171) 8 planes of the 382nd flew an AAP in the Cherbourg area from 2015 to 2220.

July 10
(#172) Lt. Brink led 8 planes of the 382nd on an AAP in the Cherbourg area from 0815 to 1000.

(#173) Lt. Knuppel led 8 P-51s of the 381st on an AAP in the Cherbourg area from 1110 to 1340.

July 11
(#174) Capt. Morrison led 8 pilots of the 380th on an AAP in the Cherbourg area from 1110 to 1305. The planes patrolled the area from 1125 to 1250.

(#175) Lt. Carter led 8 P-51s of the 381st on the

Cherbourg area from 1245 to 1435. Lt. Williams aborted with an oil leak and the rest flew an uneventful patrol.

(#176) 8 P-51s of the 382nd flew an AAP in the Cherbourg area from 1710 to 1910.

(#177) Maj. Culberson led 9 P-51s of the 381st on an AAP in the Cherbourg area from 1845 to 2100. The pilots arrived in the area at 1850 and patrolled until 2050. Lt. Edward M. Myers was hit by flak and crash-landed near Caumont where he evaded capture and returned to Allied lines in August. Several Me-109's were spotted near Falaise but no contact was made.
(1 lost)

July 12
(#178) Capt. DeLong led 8 P-51s of the 380th on an Armed Recon in the Angars-Nantes-Le Mans area from 0850 to 1130.

(#179) Capt. Brown led 12 planes of the 382nd on an Armed Recon in the Cherbourg area from 0920 to 1045. At 0954, northwest of Vitre, 10 FW-190's were engaged and the pilots downed 5 without loss.
(5-0-3 air)

Sqn		Claims
382nd:	Lt. J.W. Schmidt	(2)FW-190 dest(air)
	Lt. F. Kozaczka	FW-190 dest(air)
		FW-190 dam(air)
	Lt. R.E. Schillereff	FW-190 dest(air)
	Lt. J.H. Santarlasci	FW-190 dest(air)
	Capt. J.R. Brown	FW-190 dam(air)
	Lt. E.W. Odell	FW-190 dam(air)

(#180) Lt. Boland led 12 P-51s of the 381st on an AAP in the Angars-Nantes-Mortain-Rennes area from 0930 to 1135. The pilots patrolled without incident from 1027 to 1055.

(#181) 12 planes of the 382nd flew an Armed Recon in the Angars area from 0945 to 1145. The ships were on station from 1040 to 1100 with no problems.

(#182) 12 P-51s of the 382nd flew an Armed Recon in the Angars area from 1620 to 1745. The only claim was 0-1 loco near Brnie.

(#183) Capt. Lasko led 12 P-51s of the 381st on an AAP in the Angars-Nantes-Mortain-Rennes area from 1627 to 1812.

(#184) Capt. McEachron led 8 Mustangs of the 380th on an Armed Recon in the Angars-Nantes-Le Mans area from 1645 to 1900. A train was strafed with claims of 0-5 railcars.

(#185) Capt. Williams led 12 P-51s of the 380th on an Armed Recon in the Angars-Nantes-Le Mans area from 1710 to 2210.

July 13
(#186) Lt. Munder led 4 P-51s (the others were Lts. Williams and Richardson, and F/O Scott) of the 381st on an Armed Recon in the St. Lô area from 1010 to 1200.

(#187) Lt. Boland led 8 P-51s of the 381st on an AAP in the St. Lô area from 1545 to 1735.

July 14
(#188) 8 planes of the 382nd flew an AAP in the Cherbourg area from 0648 to 0853.

(#189) Capt. Morrison led 8 pilots of the 380th on an Armed Recon in the Tillers/Courville area from 1130 to 1310.

(#190) 8 P-51s of the 381st flew an AAP in the Cherbourg area from 1240 to 1445.

(#191) 8 pilots of the 382nd flew an AAP in the Cherbourg area from 1840 to 2040.

July 15
(#192) Capt. DeLong led 8 P-51s of the 380th on an AAP in the Cherbourg area from 0535 to 0725.

(#193) Maj. Culberson led 8 planes of the 381st on an AAP in the Cherbourg area from 0650 to 0905.

(#194) 8 P-51s of the 382nd flew an AAP in the Cherbourg area from 0810 to 1040.

(#195) Capt. Tilson led 8 P-51s of the 380th on an AAP in the Cherbourg area from 1145 to 1350.

(#196) Capt. Williams led 8 Mustangs of the 380th on an AAP in the Cherbourg area from 1805 to 2000.

(#197) Lt. Knuppel led 8 P-51s of the 381st on an AAP in the Cherbourg area from 1930 to 2200.

July 16
(#198) Lt. Munder led 9 P-51s of the 381st on a planned B-26 escort from 1210 to 1355. No R/V was made so the pilots circled the Ambriers area until heading home.

(#199) Capt. Williams led 8 P-51s of the 380th on an AAP in the St. Lô area from 1440 to 1640. Lt. James R. Anderson was lost in bad weather while F/O Eugene Murphy was hit by American ground gunners. Murphy safely crash-landed southeast of Isigny without injury but Anderson was never heard from again.

(1 lost)

(#200) 8 P-51s of the 382nd flew an AAP in the St. Lô area, times unknown.

(#201) Capt. Melancon led 8 P-51s of the 380th on an AAP in the St. Lô area from 1801 to 2001.

(#202) 9 planes of the 382nd flew an AAP in the St. Lô area from 1937 to 2140.

(#203) Lt. Boland led 9 Mustangs of the 381st on an AAP in the St. Lô area from 2151 to 2240.

July 17
(#204) Capt. DeLong led 8 P-51s of the 380th on an AAP in the Caen-Montfort area from 1550 to 1800. The pilots were vectored to Montfort but saw nothing.

July 18
(#205) Lt. McGee led 8 P-51s of the 382nd on a sweep of the Falaise-Argentan area from 0855 to 1010. Near Argentan, 35-plus Me-109's bounced the pilots, and while Lt. William E. Bullard was shot down and captured, the 382nd claimed 9 kills.

(9-0-5 air)
(1 lost)

Sqn		*Claims*
382nd:	Lt. R.B. McGee	(3)Me-109 dest(air)
	Lt. J.H. Clark	(2)Me-109 dest(air)
		(2)Me-109 dam(air)
	Lt. R.W. Asbury	Me-109 dest(air)
		(2)Me-109 dam(air)
	Lt. W.E. Bullard	Me-109 dest(air)
	Lt. E.T. Pawlak	Me-109 dest(air)

	Me-109 dam(air)
Lt. D.E. Williams	Me-109 dest(air)

(#206) Capt. Lasko led 12 P-51s of the 381st on a sweep of the Chartres-Rouen area from 1100 to 1300.

(#207) Capt. Tilson led 12 P-51s of the 380th on a sweep of the Chartres-Rouen area from 1300 to 1505. The pilots patrolled from 1336 to 1435, and while two Me-109's were seen south of Caen, nothing developed.

(#208) Lt. Asbury led 8 planes of the 382nd on a sweep of the Dreux-Rouen-Evreux area from 1435 to 1640. The pilots were vectored a number of times but nothing was seen.

(#209) Lt. Carter led 12 Mustangs of the 381st on a sweep of the Dreux-Evreux-Alencon area from 1655 to 1750. Due to weather factors, the mission was recalled at 1730 while southwest of Caen.

(#210) Capt. McEachron led 12 P-51s of the 380th on a sweep of the Chartres-Rouen area from 1855 to 2020. The pilots were vectored to St. Lô but the bandits turned out to be P-38's.

July 19
No missions were flown, but as the group diary stated, "Only excitement today was provided when the engineers decided to dynamite the old German ammunition dump back of headquarters. They added a couple Teller mines and 100 hand grenades so as to dispose of them. They did a great job of it and blew out most of the windows in headquarters as well as catapulting hunks of concrete through the S-3 door a block away. It may be rough in the ETO, but it's not dull."

July 20
(#211) 8 P-51s of the 382nd flew an AAP in the Cherbourg area from 0525 to 0715.

(#212) Lt. Munder led 8 planes of the 381st on an AAP in the Cherbourg area from 0700 to 0815. The flight was recalled and all but one pilot landed in England. These pilots took off at 1500 and arrived back at Maupertus by 1545.

(#213) 8 pilots of the 382nd flew an AAP in the Cherbourg area from 1500 to 1620. Although vectored to bogies, the only planes seen were Allied.

(#214) Maj. Culberson led 8 P-51s of the 381st on an AAP in the Cherbourg area from 1550 to 1700.

July 22
Lt. Charles R. Reddig (380th) who had been lost on July 4, returned to visit the Group after evading capture.

July 23
(#215) Lt. Knuppel led 9 P-51s of the 381st on an AAP in the Cherbourg area from 1130 to 1245. The mission was recalled early due to weather factors.

(#216) 8 pilots of the 382nd flew an AAP in the Cherbourg area from 1420 to 1630. The P-51s were vectored to bogies, but as usual, the only planes seen were friendly.

(#217)) Capt. Lasko led 8 P-51s of the 381st on an AAP in the Cherbourg area from 1600 to 1750.

(#218) Capt. Morrison led 8 planes of the 380th on an AAP in the Cherbourg area from 1727 to 1910.

(#219) 8 planes of the 382nd flew an AAP in the Cherbourg area from 1855 to 2038. Again vectored towards suspected enemy planes, only one Allied fighter was seen.

(#220) Lt. Boland led 8 Mustangs of the 381st on an AAP in the Cherbourg area from 2020 to 2210.

July 24
(#221) Col. Tipton led 36 P-51s on a sweep of the Alencon-Chartres-Argentan area from 1050 to 1415 (landings were spread out, one squadron landed at 1320, one at 1405, and one at 1415). Two pilots aborted and the rest carried out an uneventful flight.

(#222) Maj. Culberson led 37 planes on a sweep of the Chateaudun-Tours-Laval area from 1630 to 1830. F/O Scott aborted and the rest of the mission was without incident.

Another evadee, Lt. John W. Oyler (380th), returned for a visit before going back to the States. Oyler had gone down on a July 4 mission.

July 25
(#223) Capt. Morrison led 8 P-51s of the 380th on an AAP to the Bayeaux area from 0609 to 0735.

(#224) Lt. Boland led 9 Mustangs of the 381st on an AAP in the Argentan area from 0700 to 0900.

(#225) 8 P-51s of the 382nd flew an AAP in the Le Mans area from 0830 to1045.

(#226) Capt. Lasko led 24 P-51s of the 381st and 382nd on a sweep of the Rennes-Nantes-Le Mans area from 1000 to 1230. Lt. Jones (381st) had to bail out shortly after take-off and the rest of the mission was routine.

(#227) Capt. DeLong led 8 P-51s of the 380th on a sweep of the Alencon-Chartres area from 1018 to 1230.

(#228) Capt. Morrison led 35 P-51s on a sweep of the Rennes-Angars-Nantes-Le Mans area from 1455 to 1735. A 380th pilot became separated and ran into 8 FW-190's south of Le Mans. He destroyed one Focke Wulf before breaking off and heading home. One squadron chased bogies south of Le Mans which turned out to be Allied planes, while another squadron saw a Me-109 east of Le Mans which escaped.
(1-0-0 air)

Sqn		Claims
380th:	Lt. W.H. Steiner	FW-190 dest(air)

July 26
(#229) Capt. Melancon led 8 P-51s (two later aborted) of the 380th on an AAP in the Cherbourg area from 0640 to 0830.

(#230) 8 planes of the 382nd flew an AAP in the Cherbourg area from 0830 to 1050.

(#231) Capt. McEachron led 8 P-51s of the 380th on an AAP in the Cherbourg area from 1015 to 1215. The pilots saw a convoy of trucks northwest of Villedieu, but did not attack since they had red crosses on them.

(#232) Maj. Culberson led 8 planes of the 381st on an AAP in the St. Lô area from 1150 to 1340.

(#233) 7 P-51s of the 382nd flew an AAP in the Cherbourg area from 1315 to 1525.

(#234) Capt. Morrison led 8 P-51s of the 380th on an AAP in the Cherbourg area from 1450 to 1648.

(#235) Capt. Melancon led 8 planes of the 380th on an AAP in the Cherbourg area from 1625 to 1840.

(#236) Lt. Boland led 8 P-51s of the 381st on an AAP in the St. Lô-Lessay area from 1626 to 1850.

(#237) 8 P-51s of the 382nd flew an AAP in the Cherbourg area from 1805 to 2005.

(#238) Capt. Williams led 8 pilots of the 380th on an AAP in the Cherbourg area from 1940 to 2100.

(#239) 8 P-51s of the 382nd flew a B-26 escort to Dreux from 2015 to 2145. R/V was made at 2037 near Trouville and the pilots later broke in the same area at 2120.

(#240) Lt. Carter led 11 P-51s of the 381st on an AAP in the St. Lô-Lessay area from 2020 to 2200.

(#241) 8 Mustangs of the 382nd flew an AAP in the Cherbourg area from 2115 to 2225.

Also on this date, Maj. Dave H. Culberson, CO of the 381st, was killed while on a test flight in his new P-51D, "Huntin' Trouble II". Taking over as head of the 381st was Capt. Charles W. Lasko, a former 354th Fighter Group ace.
(1 killed)

July 27
(#242) Capt. McEachron led 8 P-51s of the 380th on a sweep of the Vire-Laval-Avranches area from 1324 to 1510. Two pilots aborted and one flight attacked a truck convoy with unknown results. Capt. Burl R. Williams was hit by ground fire and bailed out near Forges-A-Cambro to become a POW.
(1 lost)

(#243) Lt. Carter led 12 P-51s of the 381st on a sweep of the Alencon-Forges-Caen area from 1445 to 1715.

(#244) 12 pilots of the 382nd flew an AAP in the Avranches-Laval-Vire area from 1645 to 1740. The pilots saw 30-40 railcars near Alencon but did not make any passes.

(#245) Capt. Melancon led 12 P-51s of the 380th on a sweep of the Vire-Alencon-Avranches area from 1850 to 2105.

(#246) Capt. Tilson led 12 P-51s of the 380th on an AAP in the Laval-Vire-Avranches area from 2115 to 2225.

July 28
(#247) Lt. Boland led 12 P-51s of the 381st on an A-20 escort from 1445 to 1615. R/V was at 1457 near Cape de la Hague and the A-20's were taken to the Argentan area then later left at 1600 near the Channel.

(#248) 24 P-51s of the 380th and 382nd flew an AAP in the Argentan-Rennes area from 1700 to 1950. Numerous vectors were received but only P-47's and P-51s were seen. Returning home, Lt. Rolland (380th) was forced to belly-in but escaped injury.

(#249) Capt. Lasko led 15 P-51s of the 381st on a sweep of the Avranches area from 2015 to 2210.

July 29
(#250) Capt. Morrison led 8 P-51s of the 380th on an AAP in the St. Lô-Coutances area from 0550 to 0742.

(#251) Lt. Recagno led 8 planes of the 381st on an AAP in the Cherbourg area from 1130 to 1315. Lt. Wheeler aborted and the remaining pilots had an uneventful flight.

(#252) 8 pilots of the 382nd flew an AAP in the Cherbourg area from 1300 to 1445.

(#253) Capt. Melancon led 8 P-51s of the 380th on an AAP in the St. Lô-Coutances area from 1400 to 1520.

(#254) Lt. Boland led 12 Mustangs of the 381st on an AAP in the Cherbourg area from 1440 to 1605.

(#255) 12 planes of the 382nd flew an AAP in the Cherbourg area from 1540 to 1715.

(#256) Capt. Tilson led 11 P-51s of the 380th on an AAP in the Cherbourg area from 1730 to 1845.

(#257) Lt. Carter led 12 planes of the 381st on an AAP in the Cherbourg area from 1815 to 2015. Lt. Thoresz aborted and the rest carried out a routine patrol.

(#258) 12 pilots of the 382nd flew an AAP in the Cherbourg area from 1935 to 2135. The planes were vectored to Folligny but only some RAF Typhoons were seen.

(#259) Capt. Fletcher led 12 P-51s of the 380th on an AAP in the Cherbourg area from 2055 to 2220.

July 30
(#260) 8 planes of the 382nd flew an AAP in the Cherbourg area from 0710 to 0915.

(#261) Capt. Tilson led 8 Mustangs of the 380th on an AAP in the Cherbourg area from 0855 to 1100.

(#262) Lt. Carter led 8 planes of the 381st on an AAP in the Cherbourg area from 1030 to 1215.

(#263) 8 pilots of the 382nd flew an AAP in the Cherbourg area from 1140 to 1345.

(#264) Capt. Morrison led 8 P-51s of the 380th on an AAP in the Cherbourg area from 1310 to 1510.

(#265) Lt. Knuppel led 16 planes of the 381st on an AAP in the Cherbourg area from 1435 to 1650. A number of vehicles were seen, but all turned out to be Allied.

(#266) 16 P-51s of the 382nd flew an AAP in the Cherbourg area from 1610 to 1810.

(#267) Capt. Melancon led 12 pilots of the 380th on an AAP in the Cherbourg area from 1750 to 1950.

(#268) Lt. Recagno led 16 P-51s of the 381st on an AAP in the Cherbourg area from 1855 to 2015.

(#269) Lt. Brink led 16 planes of the 382nd on an AAP in the Cherbourg area from 2030 to 2230. One pilot aborted and the other Mustangs were repeatedly bounced by 404th Fighter Group P-47's. Fortunately, no damage was done before the Thunderbolts finally broke away.

July 31
(#270) Capt. Melancon led 12 P-51s of the 380th on a B-26 escort from 1103 to 1300. R/V was made at 1124 near Cabourg and the bombers were taken to the Tours area. Escort was later terminated at 1245 near Cabourg.

(#271) Lt. Munder led 12 planes of the 381st on an A-20 escort from 1113 to 1305. R/V was at 1140 near Villers Sur Mer and the bombers went to the Argentan/Beauzville area. Escort was later broken at 1250 near Villers Sur Mer.

(#272) 12 P-51s of the 382nd flew a B-26 escort from 1115 to 1330. R/V was made at 1150 northeast of Lisieux and the bombers went to the Chartres area.

(#273) Col. Tipton led 32 Mustangs on a sweep of the Nantes-Le Mans area from 1658 to 1905.

(#274) Capt. Lasko led 12 planes of the 381st on an A-20 escort from 1830 to 2035. R/V was at 1900 near Villers Sur Mer, the bombers hit targets in the Nantes/Gassicourt area, then the bombers were left back at Villers Sur Mer.

(#275) Lt. Recagno led 12 P-51s of the 381st on an AAP in the Granville area from 1900 to 2120.

August 1
(#276) 8 P-51s of the 382nd flew an AAP in the Avranches area from 1850 to 2105.

August 2
(#277) Capt. Tilson led 8 P-51s (one later aborted) of the 380th on an AAP in the Vitre-Rennes area from 1630 to 1830.

(#278) Lt. Brink led 8 P-51s of the 382nd on an AAP in the Avranches area from 1750 to 1945.

(#279) Capt. Fletcher led 8 planes of the 380th on an AAP in the Avranches-St. Valery area from 1906 to 2044.

(#280) Lt. Boland led 8 P-51s of the 381st on an AAP in the Avranches area from 1950 to 2105.

(#281) 8 pilots of the 382nd flew a sweep in the Avranches area from 2050 to 2220.

August 3
(#282) Capt. DeLong led 16 P-51s of the 380th on a sweep of the Avranches-Lannion-Brest area from 1700 to 1855.

(#283) Lt. Brink led 16 pilots of the 382nd on a sweep of the Avranches-Vannes-St. Briene area from 1710 to 1910.

(#284) Capt. Lasko led 8 Mustangs of the 381st on an AAP in the Rennes-Avranches area from 1850 to 2150.

August 4
(#285) Lt. Kammerlohr led 8 P-51s of the 380th on an AAP in the Rennes area from 0628 to 0734.

(#286) Lt. Gallagher led 8 planes of the 381st on an AAP in the Avranches area from 0810 to 0930.

(#287) Lt. Brink led 8 P-51s of the 382nd on an AAP in the Brest area from 1125 to 1400. Two pilots aborted and one of them, Lt. Santarlasci, bailed out near Granville after his engine quit. He returned to Maupertus later in the day.

(#288) Lt. Munder led 8 planes of the 381st on an AAP in the Avranches area from 1405 to 1650.

(#289) 8 P-51s of the 382nd flew an AAP in the Avranches-Rennes area from 1600 to 1830.

(#290) Lt. Ballinger led 8 P-51s of the 380th on an AAP in the Avranches area from 1801 to 2025.

(#291) Lt. Boland led 8 planes of the 381st on an AAP in the Avranches area from 2000 to 2200.

August 6
(#292) Lt. Reinhart led 11 P-51s of the 381st on a planned A-20 escort from 1045 to 1240. No R/V was made due to weather conditions and the pilots then patrolled the Oissel area.

(#293) 12 pilots of the 382nd flew a planned B-26 escort from 1205 to 1300. The mission was scrubbed before R/V and ten of the P-51s landed in England.

(#294) Capt. Lasko led 12 planes of the 381st on a B-26 escort from 1900 to 2100. R/V was at 1920 near Granville and the bombers were taken to the Domfront area and out, being left at 2030 near Villerville.

(#295) Capt. DeLong led 12 P-51s of the 380th on a B-26 escort from 1905 to 2100. R/V was at 1935 near Granville and the bombers were taken to Domfront and out, being left at 2040 near Trouville.

August 7

(#296) Lt. Haynes led 7 P-51s of the 380th on an Armored Column Cover mission to the Brest area from 0630 to 0835.

(#297) Lt. Gallagher led 8 P-51s of the 381st on an ACC mission to the Brest area from 0715 to 0950.

(#298) Lt. Kammerlohr led 8 ships of the 380th on an ACC mission to the Brest area from 0816 to 1029.

(#299) Lt. Knuppel led 8 P-51s of the 381st on an ACC mission to the Brest area from 0910 to 1135. The pilots strafed wagons in the Chateaulanden area with unknown results.

(#300) Lt. Jacobson led 8 P-51s of the 381st on an ACC mission to the Brest area from 1005 to 1230. Pilots strafed and claimed 1-0 truck and 5-0 autos.

(#301) Capt. Melancon led 8 pilots of the 380th on an ACC mission to the Brest area from 1100 to 1340.

(#302) Lt. Brink led 8 P-51s of the 382nd on an ACC mission to the Brest area from 1200 to 1530. Strafing netted 3-0 staff cars and 1-0 truck, all claimed by Brink.

(#303) 7 pilots of the 382nd flew an ACC mission to the Brest area from 1305 to 1535.

(#304) Capt. DeLong led 8 planes of the 380th on an ACC mission to the Brest area from 1407 to 1633.

(#305) Capt. Lasko led 8 Mustangs of the 381st on an ACC mission to the Brest area from 1505 to 1735. Strafing netted claims of 3-0 tanks, 0-1 truck, and 0-2 horse-drawn carts near Lourget.

(#306) 8 P-51s of the 382nd flew an ACC mission to the Brest area from 1607 to 1830. Claims on the flight came to 0-3 trucks near Hennebont.

(#307) Capt. Morrison led 8 P-51s of the 380th on an ACC mission to the Brest area from 1712 to 1915.

(#308) Lt. Boland led 8 ships of the 381st on an ACC mission to the Brest area from 1800 to 2100.

(#309) Lt. Brink led 8 pilots of the 382nd on an ACC mission to the Brest area from 1905 to 2140.

(#310) Capt. DeLong led 8 planes of the 380th on an ACC mission to the Brest area from 2003 to 2212.

August 8

(#311) Capt. John R. Brown led 8 P-51s of the 382nd on a sweep to Benodet Harbor from 0548 to 0800. The planes arrived at 0635 and on the first pass, Brown was hit by fire from a destroyer. He pulled off and bellied-in near Quimper and returned to Allied hands later in the month. The rest of the pilots left the area at 0730 claiming damage to one ship.

(1 lost)

(#312) Capt. Melancon led 8 P-51s of the 380th on a C-47 escort from 0700 to 1130. The flight landed in England at 0730, took off with the transport at 1030, and brought it to Maupertus. Among the passengers onboard the C-47 was Secretary of the Treasury Morgenthau.

(#313) Lt. Jacobson led 8 planes of the 381st on an ACC mission to the Brest area from 0940 to 1215.

(#314) Capt. DeLong led 8 P-51s of the 380th on an ACC mission to the Brest area from 1048 to 1335.

(#315) Lt. Brink led 8 P-51s of the 382nd on an ACC mission to the Brest area from 1150 to 1420.

(#316) Lt. Gallagher led 8 ships of the 381st on an ACC mission in the Brest area from 1250 to 1520.

(#317) Capt. Morrison led 8 P-51s of the 380th on an ACC mission to the Brest area from 1345 to 1630.

(#318) 8 Mustangs of the 382nd flew an ACC mission in the Brest area from 1450 to 1700.

(#319) Lt. McCowan led 8 planes of the 381st on an ACC mission to the Brest area from 1545 to 1820.

(#320) Capt. Melancon led 8 P-51s of the 380th on an ACC mission to the Brest area from 1645 to 1840.

(#321) Lt. Brink led 8 planes of the 382nd on an ACC mission to the Brest area from 1745 to 2010.

(#322) Lt. Williams led 8 P-51s of the 381st on an ACC mission in the Brest area from 1840 to 2120. Lt. Albert J. Reinhart was hit by flak northeast of Avranches and he was slightly injured when he bailed out near Maupertus. Some flak positions were strafed south of Vire with unknown results for the only claims. Lt. Whited had to crash-land but he emerged unhurt.

(#323) Lt. Kammerlohr led 8 P-51s of the 380th on an ACC mission to the Brest area from 1940 to 2220.

Also, Lt. Edward J. Vesely (381st) returned for a visit to the 363rd after evading capture since his loss back on June 15.

August 9
(#324) Lt. Gallagher led 8 P-51s of the 381st on an ACC mission to the Brest area from 0615 to 0825.

(#325) 8 planes of the 382nd flew an ACC mission to the Brest area from 0648 to 0915.

(#326) Capt. DeLong led 8 P-51s of the 380th on an ACC mission to the Brest area from 0748 to 1020.

(#327) Lt. Boland led 8 planes of the 381st on an ACC mission to the Brest area from 0840 to 1120.

(#328) 8 P-51s of the 382nd flew an ACC mission in the Brest area from 0948 to 1205.

(#329) Capt. Morrison led 8 P-51s of the 380th on an ACC mission to the Brest area from 1045 to 1315. One pilot aborted and the rest strafed some horse-drawn vehicles near Pleuigneau with unknown results. Capt. Morrison was hit by flak here and he bailed out near American ground troops.
(1 lost-rescued)

(#330) Lt. Williams led 8 P-51s of the 381st on an ACC mission in the Brest area from 1140 to 1400.

(#331) Lt. Brink led 8 P-51s of the 382nd on an ACC mission to the Brest area from 1248 to1440. In the zone from 1410 to 1515, strafing netted 30-0 horse-drawn carts and 2-0 autos.

(#332) Capt. Melancon led 8 P-51s on an ACC mission to the Brest area from 1348 to 1540. One pilot, Lt. Lee, aborted and the remainder flew an uneventful mission.

(#333) Lt. Jacobson led 7 P-51s of the 381st on an ACC mission to the Brest area from 1450 to 1745. In heavy strafing, pilots claimed 50-80 vehicles and 25-0 horse-drawn carts. Lt. Fuller McCowan was hit by flak and bailed out, reaching Allied lines later in the month. Lt. Henry force-landed near Morlaix, hit his head on the gunsight, and wound up in the hospital.
(1 lost)

(#334) 8 P-51s of the 382nd flew an ACC mission to the Brest area from 1548 to 1810.

(#335) Lt. Kammerlohr led 8 planes of the 380th on an ACC mission in the Brest area from 1646 to 1921.

(#336) 8 P-51s of the 381st flew an AAP in the Brest area from 1745 to 2020.

(#337) 8 pilots of the 382nd flew an ACC mission to the Brest area from 1845 to 2130. The P-51s strafed a long column of horse-drawn vehicles and trucks, destroying or damaging an unknown number.

(#338) Capt. DeLong led 8 P-51s of the 380th on an ACC mission in the Brest area from 1948 to 2215. The pilots strafed some troops and vehicles near Ploudaniel with unknown results.

August 10
(#339) Maj. McWherter led 36 P-51s on an Armed Recon in the Cambrai-Amiens area from 1115 to 1420. The pilots were in the area from 1204 to 1332, claiming 0-1 loco (by McWherter), 0-1 railcar, and 1-0 switch house, all southeast of Soissons.

(#340) Col. Tipton led 36 planes on an Armed Recon in the Paris area from 1610 to 1930. The pilots patrolled from 1700 to 1840 and some landed at other fields due to the weather.

August 11
(#341) 11 P-51s (from all three squadrons) flew an Armed Recon in the Reims-Paris area from 1153 to 1435. The pilots dive-bombed a marshalling yard at Crepy en Valus and another at Conde, claiming 0-1 loco (by Lt. Wharton, 380th), 0-6 railcars, and 0-1 oil storage tank, besides tearing up tracks.

(#342) 36 P-51s flew an Armed Recon in the Reims-Paris area from 1608 to 1940. The marshalling yards at Perenne and Hautot were attacked from 1720 with a number of hits on railcars (over 100 were seen), 1-0 switch-house, and large amounts of track torn up.

August 13
(#343) Lt. Jacobson led 8 P-51s of the 381st on an AAP in the Alencon area from 0600 to 0800. The pilots patrolled uneventfully from 0620 to 0730.

(#344) Maj. McWherter led 8 P-51s of the 382nd on an AAP in the Alencon area from 0658 to 0915. Midway through the patrol, at 0825, a dozen enemy fighters were engaged northeast of Le Mans. Lt. George J. Brooks was shot down (he evaded capture and shortly returned) while 382nd pilots claimed 4 kills.
(4-1-1 air)
(1 lost)

Sqn		Claims
382nd:	Lt. L.E. Webster	(2)FW-190 dest(air)
		Me-109 dest(air)
	Lt. W.C. Littlefield	FW-190 dest(air)
	Lt. D.E. Frye	FW-190 prob(air)
		Me-109 dam(air)

(#345) Lt. Kammerlohr led 8 P-51s of the 380th on an AAP in the Alencon area from 0814 to 1002. The pilots patrolled from 0845 to 0945 without incident.

(#346) Lt. Pressnall led 8 planes of the 381st on an AAP in the Alencon area from 0900 to 1145. The pilots were vectored to Argentan but no enemy planes were seen.

(#347) 8 P-51s of the 382nd flew an AAP in the Alencon area from 0955 to 1130. Patrolling from 1120 to 1115, both Lt. Chester H. Rice and Lt. Dell P. Hudson were lost for unknown reasons. They were last heard from in the Argentan-Troh area strafing a convoy. Over 100 horse-drawn vehicles were attacked but exact results were not known.
(2 lost)

(#348) Capt. Melancon led 8 P-51s of the 380th on an AAP in the Alencon area from 1056 to 1305. A convoy was attacked east of Le Mans for claims of 2-0 trucks.

(#349) Capt. Lasko led 8 planes of the 381st on an AAP in the Alencon area from 1200 to 1345.

(#350) Lt. Brink led 8 ships of the 382nd on an AAP in the Alencon area from 1258 to 1454.

(#351) Lt. Haynes led 8 planes of the 380th on an AAP in the Alencon area from 1347 to 1524.

(#352) Lt. Shea led 8 P-51s of the 381st on an AAP in the Alencon area from 1500 to 1705.

(#353) 8 pilots of the 382nd flew an AAP in the Alencon area from 1558 to 1816.

(#354) Lt. Clough led 8 P-51s of the 380th on an AAP in the Alencon area from 1701 to 1925.

(#355) Lt. Munder led 8 ships of the 381st on an AAP in the Alencon area from 1800 to 2005.

(#356) Lt. Heberlein led 8 Mustangs of the 382nd on an AAP in the Alencon area from 1858 to 2115. Between Le Chopelle le Rotren and St. Cosme, 25-plus German fighters were engaged and in the 363rd's last aerial combat, pilots claimed 8 kills without loss.
(8-2-2 air)

Sqn		Claims
382nd:	Lt. E.W. Odell	(2)Me-109 dest(air)
	Lt. R.M. Heberlein	Me-109 dest(air)
		Me-109 dam(air)
	Lt. J. Jabara	FW-190 dest(air)
		Me-109 dam(air)
	Lt. W.C. Littlefield	Me-109 dest(air)
	Lt. G.E. Reeves	Me-109 dest(air)
	Lt. B.R. Underwood	Me-109 dest(air)
		Me-109 prob(air)
	Lt. L.E. Webster	FW-190 dest(air)
	F/O E.W. Fogelquist	Me-109 prob(air)

(#357) Lt. Kammerlohr led 8 P-51s of the 380th on an AAP in the Alencon area from 1954 to 2155.

August 14
(#358) Capt. Morrison led 8 planes of the 380th on an AAP in the Le Mans area from 0930 to 1130.

(#359) Lt. Pressnall led 8 ships of the 381st on an AAP in the Le Mans area from 1020 to 1240.

(#360) 8 P-51s of the 382nd flew an AAP in the Le Mans area from 1108 to 1315.

(#361) Lt. Haynes led 8 pilots of the 380th on an AAP in the Le Mans area from 1210 to 1420.

(#362) Lt. Boland led 8 P-51s of the 381st on an AAP in the Le Mans area from 1308 to 1530.

(#363) 8 planes of the 382nd flew an AAP in the Le Mans area from 1405 to 1630.

(#364) Capt. Melancon led 8 P-51s of the 380th on an AAP in the Le Mans area from 1510 to 1720.

(#365) Capt. Fletcher, Group Operations Officer, led 8 P-51s of the 381st on an AAP in the Le Mans area from 1610 to 1815.

(#366) 8 Mustangs of the 382nd flew an AAP in the Le Mans area from 1709 to 1914.

(#367) Lt. Clough led 8 planes of the 380th on an AAP in the Le Mans area from 1805 to 2025.

(#368) Lt. Munder led 8 P-51s of the 381st on an AAP in the Le Mans area from 1915 to 2135.

August 15
(#369) Capt. Melancon led 8 P-51s of the 380th on an AAP in the Nantes area from 0624 to 0815.

(#370) Lt. Pressnall led 8 pilots of the 381st on an AAP in the Dreux-Chartres area from 0700 to 0945.

(#371) 8 planes of the 382nd flew an AAP in the Dreux-Chartres area from 0750 to 1012.

(#372) Lt. Kammerlohr led 8 P-51s of the 380th on an AAP in the Nantes area from 0903 to 1112.

(#373) Lt. Tucker led 8 Mustangs of the 381st on an AAP in the Dreux-Chartres area from 0950 to 1205.

(#374) 8 P-51s of the 382nd flew an AAP in the Dreux-Chartres area from 1110 to 1330.

(#375) Capt. Morrison led 8 P-51s of the 380th on an AAP in the Nantes area from 1153 to 1405. The planes were vectored to Alencon but only friendlies were seen.

(#376) Lt. Pressnall led 8 pilots of the 381st on an AAP in the Dreux-Chartres area from 1250 to 1540.

(#377) 8 P-51s of the 382nd flew an AAP in the Dreux-Chartres area from 1402 to 1605.

(#378) Capt. Melancon led 8 P-51s of the 380th on a P-47 cover mission from 1446 to 1710. R/V was made at 1550 in the Orgeres/Chartres area and the 47's were later left at 1620 near A-13.

(#379) Capt. Lasko led 8 planes of the 381st on a P-47 cover from 1530 to 1845. R/V was at 1605 near Bayesit and the Thunderbolts hit targets in the Chartres area.

(#380) Col. Tipton led 8 P-51s of the 382nd on a planned P-47 cover from 1617 to 1842. No R/V was made so the planes patrolled the Le Mans area from 1625 to 1820.

(#381) Capt. Fletcher led 8 P-51s of the 380th on a planned P-47 cover from 1700 to 1906. Again, no R/V was made so the pilots patrolled the Paris area from 1745 to 1840.

(#382) Lt. Pressnall led 8 P-51s of the 381st on a P-47 escort from 1740 to 2030. R/V was at 1820 near Bayeaux, the 373rd Fighter Group P-47's were taken to the Chartres area, then escort was broken at 2020 near Caen.

(#383) 8 P-51s of the 382nd flew a P-47 escort from 1825 to 2014. R/V was made east of Bayeaux but the mission was scrubbed at 1955.

August 16
(#384) Col. Tipton led 36 P-51s on a sweep of the Tours-Poiters-Lineges area from 0800 to 1115. Two planes aborted and the rest swept the region from 0900 to 1015. Only 11 pilots landed at Maupertus as the rest landed on fields in England or on the Continent. Lt. Robinson (380th) ran out of fuel and crash-landed at Maupertus but was uninjured. The majority of pilots who landed elsewhere returned by 1815.

Also on this date, Lt. Fuller McCowan (381st) returned to the Group. He had been MIA since August 9 but successfully evaded.

August 17
(#385) Lt. Pressnall led 11 P-51s of the 381st on an AAP in the Chartres-Melun area from 1445 to 1715.

(#386) Lt. Kammerlohr led 12 planes of the 380th on a sweep of the Etampes area from 1735 to 2015. The only claim was for 1-0 truck near Etampes, shared by Lts. Lavin and Schubert. The day also saw two more evaders return, as Capt. John R. Brown (382nd) and Lt. Paul F. Clark (381st) paid a visit. Brown had been lost on August 8 while Clark went down back on June 24.

August 18
(#387) Lt. Haynes led 12 P-51s of the 380th on an AAP in the Nantes-Melun area from 1150 to 1415.

(#388) 12 P-51s of the 382nd flew an AAP in the Paris area from 1350 to 1635.

(#389) Col. Tipton led 12 planes of the 381st on a P-47 escort from 1530 to 1850. R/V was at 1540 and the Thunderbolts hit targets near Melun. Escort was later broken near Caen at 1820.

(#390) Capt. Morrison led 12 P-51s of the 380th on a P-47 escort from 1630 to 2017. R/V was made at 1643 and the 47's were later left at 1800 in the Nantes area.

(#391) 12 planes of the 382nd flew a P-47 escort from 1732 to 1954. Top cover was given in the Chartres area from 1825 to 1917.

(#392) Capt. Lasko led 8 P-51s of the 381st on a P-47 escort from 1820 to 2100. R/V was at 1845 and the Thunderbolts were taken to the Paris area.

August 19
A down day for the 363rd and another evader returned. Lt. Charles L. Moore (380th) had been lost on April 30 and successfully hid for three and a half months.

August 20
(#393) Col. Tipton led 13 P-51s of the 382nd on an AAP in the Argentan-Dreux area from 1455 to 1720. One pilot aborted and the rest flew an uneventful patrol.

(#394) Lt. Haynes led 12 Mustangs of the 380th on a P-47 cover from 1600 to 1750. Escort was given to the Vernon area without incident.

(#395) Lt. Gallagher led 12 P-51s of the 381st on an AAP in the Versailles-Gassicourt area from 1645 to 1900. One pilot aborted and the remainder flew a patrol from 1730 to 1830.

Cpl. James L. Cain and Pvt. Hugh L. Knight (382nd) were hospitalized with injuries resulting from souvenir hunting. While looking through German equipment still lying south of the field, the pair set off an explosion which seriously wounded them.

August 22
(#396) Lt. Kammerlohr led 12 planes of the 380th on a P-47 cover from 1645 to 1921. The 405th Fighter Group Thunderbolts were escorted from 1800 to 1815 in the Melun-Montanges area then pilots headed for home at 1840.

(#397) Capt. Munder led 12 planes of the 381st on an AAP in the Melun-Montanges area from 1745 to 2030.

(#398) Col. Tipton led 12 P-51s of the 382nd on an AAP in the Melun-Montanges area from 1747 to 1950. Some 50 horse-drawn vehicles were strafed near Melun and an unknown number were left burning.

Also on this day, an advance party left Maupertus to begin the move to the 363rd's new home at A-7, Azeville, France. Rumors also began to circulate about the future of the Group. Some said the 363rd was going home, others that it was to become a Tactical Recon outfit. The rumors were soon made fact when personnel were told that shortly the 363rd would indeed become a Recon unit.

By the summer of 1944, Allied forces were progressing through France at a steady pace. The 9th Air Force had two Recon Groups, the 10th and 67th (equipped with F-5 and F-6 aircraft), but these were not enough to meet the demand of the ground troops. Consequently, it was decided to disband an already existing unit to facilitate getting a new Recon Group into action. The 9th was also in the process of converting all its fighter groups to P-47's, these being deemed more suitable for ground support operations (even the famous 354th Fighter Group was forced to switch over for a time in late 1944 - early 1945). With only two Mustang units to choose from, and the 354th having compiled an outstanding record it was decided the 363rd would be disbanded.

August 23
(#399) Lt. Gallagher led 12 P-51s of the 381st on an AAP in the Sens area from 1030 to 1330.

(#400) 12 planes of the 382nd flew an AAP in the Nantes-Rouen area from 1315 to 1615. The pilots were in the zone from 1400 to 1520 and claimed 5-8 horse-drawn vehicles near Louviers and 0-1 flak tower south of Elbeu.

(#401) Lt. Messer led 4 P-51s of the 380th (the others were Lts. Lavin, Graham and MacDonald) on an AAP in the Nantes-Rouen area from 1333 to 1558.

(#402) Col. Tipton led 16 P-51s of the 380th and 381st on an AAP in the Nantes-Rouen area from 1435 to 1730.

(#403) 24 P-51s (from all squadrons) flew an AAP in the Nantes-Rouen area from 1700 to 1935.

Maj. Robert C. McWherter was sent home on leave and taking over as 382nd CO was Capt. Robert B. McGee

August 26
(#404) Col. Tipton led 21 planes on a sweep of the Amiens-Lille area from 0430 to 0750. The pilots never assembled as a group due to darkness so the squadrons carried out separate sweeps. Claims were 1-0 loco, 4-10 railcars, and 2-0 trucks, all shared by Capt. Munder and Lt. Newman (381st) east of Amiens, while 380th pilots claimed 1-0 loco (Lt. Bevans) and 0-5 railcars (Lt. Schriber).

(#405) 27 P-51s flew a sweep of the Amiens-Lille area from 0953 to 1220.

(#406) 27 Mustangs flew a sweep of the Amiens-Lille area from 1740 to 2040. Lt. Myles R. Nielsen (380th) was hit by flak near Breuteuil and bellied-in northwest of Vernon.
(1 lost)

August 27
(#407) 16 P-51s of the 380th and 382nd flew a sweep of the Chalon-Juvincourt area from 0757 to 1105.

(#408) Capt. Munder led 12 planes of the 381st on a B-26 escort from 1130 to 1300. R/V was at 1150 near Louviers, the bombers went to the Rouen area, then were left at 1215 near St. Valery.

(#409) Capt. Fletcher led 22 P-51s (from all squadrons) on a sweep of the Reims area from 1720 to 2000. Patrolling from 1755 to 1835, the 380th claimed 1-0 loco as a unit, plus 1-0 railcar (Lt. Sparer), 2-0 trucks (one by Fletcher and one shared by Lt. Evans and Lt. Robinson), and 0-1 flak tower.

A number of command changes took place on this date, including Col. Tipton being replaced as CO. Taking over the 363rd was Col. James M. Smelley, the new Tactical Recon Group CO. In the 382nd, Capt. McGee was sent home and taking charge was Capt. Douglas H. Buskey, while in the 381st, Capt. Lasko was given leave and his spot was filled by Capt. Fred A. Munder.

Also, Lt. Donald M. Lewis (382nd), who had been lost on April 5, returned for a visit after evading for four months.

August 28
(#410) 24 P-51s flew a sweep of the Laon-St. Quentin area from 0730 to 1030. In the area from 0800 to 0930, pilots claimed 1-0 loco north of Bestrees, 0-1 loco and 12-15 vehicles south of St. Quentin, 22-26 trucks near Marle, 6-19 trucks near Montcornet, and 1-0 gun position near St. Quentin. Lt. Augustus di Zerega (381st) was hit by flak while strafing a train, bailed out, and later returned to Allied control. He was also the last loss suffered by the 363rd Fighter Group.
(1 lost)

August 29
(#411) 28 pilots took off at 0615 for a planned sweep. Due to the weather, the mission was scrubbed and the planes landed by 0720.

August 30 - September 4
The Group was ordered to stand down to be reorganized and at midnight on the 4th, the 363rd Fighter Group ceased to exist. Before this, however, two more evaders returned for a visit: on the 31st, Lt. Edward M. Myers (381st) showed up after having

been lost on July 11; and on September 2, Lt. John A. Sharrock (380th) returned, having gone down back on April 22.

While most of the ground personnel stayed on with the 363rd Tactical Recon Group, all but three pilots were sent home or scattered among 8th and 9th Air Force units. Most of the planes remained, being field converted to recon ships. Eventually, however, these were replaced with new F-6 Mustangs.

To bring a close to the history, the group diary recorded, "Tonight at midnight we cease to be the 363 Fighter Group. The trials, tribulations, and successes of the second ranking fighter group of the Ninth Air Force will come to a halt. Tomorrow brings a different job with different duties. Here's hoping it will be even better than it has in the past."

From February through August of 1944, the 363rd flew some 411 combat missions; 107 as Group strength and 304 as individual Squadrons (101 by the 380th, 102 by the 381st, and 101 by the 382nd). In addition to claiming 88-12-50 enemy planes in aerial combat, the pilots also claimed 26-62 aircraft on the ground, 5-0 V-1's, 73-17 locos, 139-207 railcars, 224-231 vehicles, 13-5 tanks, 6-32 bridges, 2-12 boats, 2-20 flak towers, and numerous other targets destroyed or damaged.

On the debit side, 82 pilots were lost on missions, 3 were rescued from the Channel, 4 were taken off operations due to wounds or injuries, one was captured while on detached service in Italy, and 11 died in accidents, both in the States and overseas.

Broken down, the losses looked like this:

	KIA	POW	EVADERS	MIA	ASR	WIA(Off Ops)	Total
HdQts	0	0	0	0	0	0	0
380th	7	13	6	3	2	0	31
381st	18	7	6	3	1	3	38
382nd	16	4	5	5	0	1	31
Grand Total	**41**	**24**	**17**	**11**	**3**	**4**	**100**

Appendices

Appendix 1
363rd Fighter Group Totals

Month	Missions	A/C Dispatched	A/C Aborts	MIA*	Claims Air	Claims Grd
February	4	147	14	0	0-0-0	0-0
March	14	510	81	15	3-1-3	0-0
April	24	1164	140	21	13-2-9	3-14
May	27	1055	75	12	24-5-13	22-48
June	70	1698	47	20	21-1-14	1-0
July	136	1418	17	9	15-0-8	0-0
August	136	1416	9	8	12-3-3	0-0
Totals	**411**	**7408**	**383**	**85**	**88-12-50**	**26-62**

* Includes aircraft lost where the pilot was picked up by ASR

Appendix 2
Total Bomb Tonnage

Month	Tonnage	
February	nil	
March	29,500 lbs	(all 500 lb bombs)
April	157,500 lbs	(23,500 of 250 lb bombs)
		(134,000 of 500 lb bombs)
May	59,250 lbs	(18,250 of 250 lb bombs)
		(41,000 of 500 lb bombs)
June	890,260 lbs	(32,760 of 20 lb frag bombs)
		(857,500 of 500 lb bombs)
July	30,000 lbs	(all 500 lb bombs)
August	19,250 lbs	(all 250 lb bombs)
	1,185,760 lbs total	(32,760 of 20 lb frag bombs)
		(61,000 of 250 lb bombs)
		(1,092,000 of 500 lb bombs)

Appendix 3
363rd Fighter Group Organizational Set-Up

Group Commanders

LtCol. John R. Ulricson	March 1, 1943-April 8, 1943
Capt. Dave H. Culberson	April 8, 1943-April 28, 1943
Maj. Theodore C. Bunker	April 28, 1943-June 4, 1943
Col. John R. Ulricson	June 4, 1943-May 7, 1944
Col. James B. Tipton	May 7, 1944-August 9, 1944
LtCol. Ben S. Irvin	August 9, 1944-August 14, 1944
Col. James B. Tipton	August 14, 1944-August 27, 1944

Deputy Group Commanders

Maj. Marshall Cloke	May 1943-March 30, 1944
LtCol. Ben S. Irvin	March 30, 1944-August 27, 1944

Group Operations Officers

Capt. Irwin H. Dregne	March 1943-May 1943
Maj. Raleigh M. Thomason	May 24, 1943-June 22, 1944
Capt. Robert C. Fletcher	June 22, 1944-August 28, 1944
Capt. Harry M. Sample	August 28, 1944-September 4, 1944

Assistant Group Operations Officers

Capt. Dave H. Culberson	March 19, 1943-April 8, 1943
Lt. Raymond R. Wisner	November 1943-May 1944
Lt. Dell P. Hudson	November 1943-July 1944
Lt. Robert D. Kunz	June 1944-August 1944
Capt. Harry M. Sample	July 1944-August 28, 1944

380th Fighter Squadron Commanders

Capt. Evan M. McCall	March 1943-April 21, 1943
Maj. Evan M. McCall	May 24, 1943-March 30, 1944
Maj. Marshall Cloke	March 30, 1944-July 1, 1944
Capt. Louis D. Morrison	July 1, 1944-August 9, 1944
Capt. Alex J. Melancon	August 9, 1944-August 14, 1944
Capt. Louis D. Morrison	August 14, 1944-August 28, 1944

381st Fighter Squadron Commanders

Capt. Dave H. Culberson	March 1, 1943-April 8, 1943
Maj. Dave H. Culberson	May 24, 1943-July 26, 1944
Capt. Charles W. Lasko	July 26, 1944-August 27, 1944
Capt. Fred A. Munder	August 27, 1944-August 29, 1944

382nd Fighter Squadron Commanders

Lt. Thomas L. Hayes	March 1, 1943-May 1943
Maj. Robert C. McWherter	May 24, 1943-August 23, 1944
Capt. Robert B. McGee	August 23, 1944-August 27, 1944
Capt. Douglas H. Buskey	August 27, 1944-August 31, 1944

380th Fighter Squadron Operations

Capt. Martin L. DeLong	August 5, 1943-March 30, 1944
Maj. Evan M. McCall	March 30, 1944-July 1, 1944
Lt. William W. Huff	July 1, 1944-September 4, 1944

381st Fighter Squadron Operations

Capt. George R. Doerr	August 1943-April 22, 1944
Capt. James B. Dalglish	April 23, 1944-June 29, 1944
Capt. Jeremiah M. Boland	June 29, 1944-August 16, 1944
Capt. Fred A. Munder	August 16, 1944-August 27, 1944
Lt. Lloyd E. Wheeler	August 27, 1944-September 4, 1944

382nd Fighter Squadron Operations

Lt. James N. Brink	August 1943-March 25, 1944
Capt. Louis D. Morrison	March 25, 1944-July 1, 1944
Capt. John R. Brown	July 1, 1944-August 8, 1944
Lt. Ray E. Schillereff	August 8, 1944-August 27, 1944

Wing Assignments

70th Ftr Wing, IX Ftr Command	December 1943-April 1944
100th Ftr Wing, XIX ASC, IX Ftr Command	April 1944-July 4, 1944
84th Ftr Wing, IX TAC, IX Ftr Command	July 4, 1944-July 14, 1944
100th Ftr Wing, XIX TAC, IX Ftr Command	July 14, 1944-September 4, 1944

Appendix 4
363rd Fighter Group Claims

	AIR			GRD	
	Destroyed	**Probable**	**Damaged**	**Destroyed**	**Damaged**
HdQts	1	0	1	1	0
380th	30	3	21	0	0
381st	15	4	8	9	36
382nd	42	5	20	16	26
Totals	**88**	**12**	**50**	**26**	**62**

Appendix 5
Claims by Enemy Aircraft Type

	AIR			GRD	
	Destroyed	**Probable**	**Damaged**	**Destroyed**	**Damaged**
Me-109	49	8	24	2	3
FW-190	31	3	19	0	4
Me-410	7	0	6	0	0
Bu-181	1	0	0	0	0
Ju-88	0	1	1	8	7
He-111	0	0	0	5	15
Trainers	0	0	0	5	16
He-177	0	0	0	2	2
Do-217	0	0	0	1	0
FW-200	0	0	0	1	0
Me-110	0	0	0	1	0
BV-222	0	0	0	1	0
u/i a/c	0	0	0	0	9
He-115	0	0	0	0	4
Ju-52	0	0	0	0	1
Glider	0	0	0	0	1

Appendix 6
363rd Fighter Group Scorers

Headquarters

	Air	Grd	
B.S. Irvin	0-0-1	0-0	
J.B. Tipton	1-0-0	1-0	

380th Fighter Squadron

	Air	Grd	
B.W. Carr	1-0-0	0-0	later 14 air w/354th Ftr Grp
G.C. Clough	1-0-0	0-0	
M. Cloke	2-0-1	0-0	
R.C. Fletcher	1-0-1	0-0	
W.M. Haynes	1-0-0	0-0	
N.D. Hersberger	0-0-0.5	0-0	
J.E. Hill	2-0-2	0-0	
M.A. Kammerlohr	1-0-1	0-0	
T.S.L. McClung	1-0-0	0-0	
G.T. McEachron	3-1-3	0-0	
A.J. Melancon	1-0-0	0-0	
H.B. Messer	0-0.5-0	0-0	
A.W. Owen	1-1-3	0-0	
D.W. Ray	1-0-0	0-0	
C.R. Reddig	1-0-0	0-0	
L.F. Reetzke	0-0-4	0-0	
J.A. Sharrock	1-0-1.5	0-0	
W.H. Steiner	4-0-0	0-0	plus 382nd Ftr Sqn
T.J. Tilson	3-0-0	0-0	
B.W. Turner	1-0-0	0-0	
R.J. Tyler	0-0.5-0	0-0	
E.E. Vance	2-0-1	0-0	
B.R. Williams	2-0-3	0-0	

381st Fighter Squadron

	Air	Grd	
E.H. Berglind	0-1-0	0-0	
J.M. Boland	1-0-1	0-0	
D.H. Culberson	2-0-2	0-0	
J.B. Dalglish	1-0-0	0-0	plus 8 air w/ 354th Ftr Grp later 0.5 air w/354th Ftr Grp
C.H. Davis	0-0-0	1.25-4.5	
R.D. Freyermuth	0-0-0	3.25-4.5	

	Air	Grd	
P.H. Henry	2-0-0	0-0	
H.R. Howell	2-0-0	0-0	
V.T. Johnson	0-0-1	0-0	
R.P. Lucas	0-0-1	0-0	
H.D. Knuppel	0-1-1	0-0	
A.M. Mimler	0-2-0	1-0	
A.J. Reinhart	0-0-0	0-1	later 2 air w/36th Ftr Grp
W.R. Schmidt	3-0-0	1.25-7.5	
C.E. Shea	0-0-0	0.25-4.5	
C.H. Smith	0-0-1	0-8	
L.D. Smutz	0-0-0	0-2	
W.W. Steinke	1-0-0	0-0	
D.R. Tucker	0-0-0	1-4	
W.A. Webb	1-0-0	0-0	
P.W. Wood	2-0-0	0-0	
W.H. Yochim	0-0-1	0-0	

382nd Fighter Squadron

	Air	Grd	
R.W. Asbury	1.5-0-3	0-0	later 3.5 air w/354th Ftr Grp
D.L. Boatright	0-0-1	1-0	
J.N. Brink	1-0-1	0-0	
J.R. Brown	0-0-1	4-8	
W.E. Bullard	1-0-0	1-1	
J.H. Clark	2-0-2	4-1	
E.W. Fogelquist	0-1-0	0-0	
D.E. Frye	0-1-1	0-0	
R.M. Heberlein	1-0-2	0-0	
J. Jabara	1.5-1-1	0-0	later 5.5 grd w/355th Ftr Grp
D.L. King	1-1-1	0-0	later 4 air w/ 373rd Ftr Grp
F. Kozaczka	1-0-1	0-2	later 2 air w/354th Ftr Grp
W.C. Littlefield	2-0-0	0-0	later 1 air w/ 354th Ftr Grp
R.B. McGee	4-0-0	0-0	
R.C. McWherter	3-0-0	0-0	plus 1 air w/ 17th Pur Sqn, PTO
L.D. Morrison	1-0-0	0-1	

E.W. Odell	2-0-1	1-0			W.H. Steiner	0-0-0	1-2	plus 380th Ftr Sqn
E.T. Pawlak	1-0-1	0-0			J.R. Stricker	1-0-0	1-1	
R.E. Proctor	0-0-1	0-2			M.A. Thompson	2.5-0-1	0-0	
G.E. Reeves	1-0-0	0-0			B.R. Underwood	1-1-0	0-0	later 1 air
J. Robertson	1-0-0	0-4						w/406th Ftr Grp
D.H. Rook	0-0-0	1-1			L.E. Webster	4-0-1	0-2	
J.H. Santarlasci	3-0-1	0-0			D.E. Williams	1-0-0	0-0	
R.E. Schillereff	1-0-0	2-1			H.A. Winham	0.5-0-0	0-0	
J.W. Schmidt	3-0-0	0-0						

Appendix 7
Pilot List

The following pages contain a list of pilots assigned to the 363rd Fighter Group from March of 1943 through September 4, 1944. Information for each pilot includes (where known) his last rank with the 363rd, serial number, dates of service, fate (POW, MIA, etc.), number of missions and/or combat hours, personal aircraft, and groundcrew.

The reader will notice a fairly large number of pilots joined the unit in February of 1944, having been sent from the 365th Fighter Group. The reason for this was the fact that the 365th did not need P-51 trained pilots, as it flew P-47's. Also, a reason given comes from one of the men involved, who stated the pilots in question did not want to fly P-47's either. After dragging their feet in transitioning, the 365th CO said, "ENOUGH!", and promptly shipped them to the 363rd.

Other replacements trickled into the Group through March, April, and May, covering losses and transfers. In June, another large batch of replacements arrived, mainly former instructors from the States. July and August also saw a number of transfers to fill holes left not only from losses, but in some "old-timers" finishing their tours and going home. The author has tried to record the eventual assignment (combat) of the pilots left when the 363rd was broken-up; however, the task is not 100% complete. Quite a few of the high-time pilots went back to the States and remained there, though some did return for second tours with different units. The remaining pilots went mainly to the P-51 equipped 354th Fighter Group or 9th Weather Recon Squadron or scattered P-47 groups of the 9th Air Force. At least two (Eugene Murphy and James Jabara) ended up with 8th Air Force P-51 groups and one pilot, John Brown, eventually wound up in the Pacific flying P-47N's against Japan.

Headquarters

Cloke, Marshall, Maj.
(0-23310)

May 1943-March 1944; to 380th Ftr Sqn

Culberson, Dave H., Maj.
(0-431126)

March 1943-April 1943; to 381st Ftr Sqn

Dregne, Irwin H., Capt.
(0-431399)

March 1943-April 1943; to 357th Ftr Grp
and later claimed 10.5 air/ground kills in ETO

Fletcher, Robert C., Capt.
(0-732207)

June 1944-August 1944; ex-380th Ftr Sqn

Hudson, Dell P., Lt.
(0-748657)

November 1943-July 1944; to 382nd Ftr Sqn

Irvin, Ben S., LtCol.
(0-399532)

March 1944-August 1944; ex-17th Pur Sqn, PTO
and 362nd Ftr Grp, ETO
27 missions
P-51D C3- 44-13575

Kunz, Robert D., Lt.
(0-748689)

June 1944-August 1944; ex-382nd Ftr Sqn
later 405th Ftr Grp and KIA 11-26-44
P-51D C3- "El Don"

Sample, Harry M., Capt.
(0-664061)

July 1944-August 1944; ex-380th Ftr Sqn
later 371st Ftr Grp and KIA 10-29-44

Thomason, Raleigh M., Maj.
(0-399585)

May 1943-June 1944; possibly flew in Pacific
Theater and not known to have flown in ETO

Tipton, James B., Col.
(0-22554)

May 1944-September 1944; later to 358th Ftr Grp
and claimed 1 kill; ex-366th Ftr Grp
28 missions
P-51D A9- 44-13805 "Diablo"
S/Sgt. Ollie P. Stone-c/c
Sgt. Ralph C. Fritz-ac/c
Cpl. William H. Evans-arm.

Ulricson, John R., Col.
(0-20783)

March 1943-April 1943
June 1943-May 1944; to IX Ftr Cmd HdQts
25 missions
P-51B A9-J 43-6716 "Lolita"

Wisner, Raymond R., Lt.
(0-745559)

November 1943-May 1944; to 380th Ftr Sqn,
ex-381st Ftr Sqn

380th Fighter Squadron

Anderson, James R., Lt. (0-698089)	June 1944-July 16, 1944(KIA)
Andrews, James K., Lt. (0-689184)	June 1944-September 1944
Ballinger, Edward P., Capt. (0-748517)	August 1943-August 1944; to States P-51B A9- "Angel's Playmate" P-51B A9- "Angel's Playmate II" P-51B A9- "Angel's Playmate III" P-51D A9- 44-13587 "Angel's Playmate IV"
Barlow, James E., Lt. (0-748519)	November 1943-April 23, 1944(POW) ex-382nd Ftr Sqn
Benson, Roy, Jr., Lt. (0-804989)	August 1943-May 11, 1944(POW) 23 missions P-51B A9-R 43-6950 S/Sgt. Alvin J. Wolff-c/c Sgt. Robert E. Watson-ac/c
Bevans, Douglas O., Lt. (0-731925)	June 1944-September 1944
Black, Harry A., Lt. (0-1166672)	June 1944-September 1944; to 358th Ftr Grp 1 mission
Bruce, Lloyd M., Lt. (0-804106)	August 1943-May 11, 1944(POW)
Carr, Bruce W., F/O (T-61258)	February 1944-May 1944; to 354th Ftr Grp and later 14 air and 11.5 grd; ex-365th Ftr Grp
Carter, Lloyd C., Lt. (0-744543)	August 1943-October 1943; to 360th Ftr Grp
Casadont, Lawrence, Lt. (0-748584)	August 1943-October 21, 1943(KIAc)
Cashio, Carlos J., Lt. (0-793584)	August 1943-November 1943; to 369th Ftr Grp
Clemovitz, Feodor, Lt. (0-749528)	August 1943-May 28, 1944(POW) P-51B A9- "Little Joe"

Cloke, Marshall, Maj.
(0-23310)

March 1944-July 1944; ex-HdQts
33 missions; later 354th Ftr Grp

Clough, Gerald C., Capt.
(0-886260)

January 1944-September 1944
76 missions, 212 hours
P-51B A9-A "Corky-Anne"
P-51D A9-A 44-13765 "Corky-Anne II"
S/Sgt. Wallace W. Winkler-c/c
S/Sgt. Jess W. Foster-ac/c
Cpl. John C. Hackett-arm.

Cole, Gardner E., Lt.
(0-414486)

August 1944-September 1944; to 362nd Ftr
Grp and claimed 1 kill before POW 3-22-45
2 missions

DeLong, Martin L., Maj.
(0-791289)

July 1943-August 1944; to States
P-51B A9- "Southern Belle"
P-51D A9- 44-13606 "Southern Belle II"
S/Sgt. Jack J. Kellar-c/c
Sgt. Tom F. Hanley-ac/c
Sgt. Clare H. McGlynn-arm.

Dimmock, Charles A., Lt.
(0-706366)

July 1944-September 1944; to 36th Ftr Grp
and KIA 11-7-44

Diya, Daniel G., F/O
(T-61260)

February 1944-April 29, 1944(MIA-E)
ex-365th Ftr Grp

Evans, George W., Jr., Lt.
(0-668325)

June 1944-September 1944; to 36th Ftr Grp

Ferris, Robert L., Lt.
(0-707678)

June 1944-September 1944

Firkins, Hugh F., F/O
(T-122256)

June 1944-September 1944

Fletcher, Robert C., Capt.
(0-732207)

March 1944-June 1944; to HdQts

Fontes, Alfred, Lt.
(0-800115)

August 1943-April 8, 1944(POW)

Fryer, Earl R., Lt.
(0-805025)

August 1943-November 1943; to 328th Ftr Grp
later in ETO w/55th Ftr Grp and claimed 5 air-
ground kills before KIA 11-8-44

Graham, Walter W., Lt.   June 1944-September 1944
(0-680023)

Hale, Thomas E., Lt.   August 1943-March 29, 1944(KIAc)
(0-805035)   P-51B A9-U 43-6817

Hardin, James M., Lt.   June 1944-September 1944
(0-668448)

Harrold, Paul C., Lt.   June 1944-September 1944; to 36th Ftr Grp
(0-678042)

Haynes, William M., Capt.   August 1943-August 1944; to States
(0-805044)   P-51B A9- "Windy City"
                                      P-51B A9- "Windy City II"
                                      P-51B A9- 43-6524 "Windy City III"
                                      P-51D A9- 44-13550 "Windy City IV"
                                      S/Sgt. Anthony H. Haley-c/c
                                      Cpl. Stanley J. Boron-arm.

Hersberger, Norman D., Lt.   August 1943-April 29, 1944(POW)
(0-805045)

Hill, James E., Lt.   August 1943-June 14, 1944(POW)
(0-805048)   159 hours
                                      P-51B A9-Z 42-106795 "Georgia Ann"
                                      Cpl. Harry O. Gentry-arm.

Holland, William D., Lt.   July 1944-September 1944; to 36th Ftr Grp
(0-886028)   and KIA 1-30-45

Hollowell, Maurice W., Lt.   June 1944-June 12, 1944(KIA)
(0-668464)

Huff, William W., Lt.   June 1944-September 1944
(0-664009)   P-51B A9- 43-7010
                                      S/Sgt. Mike Salvage-c/c
                                      Sgt. Sol W. Malin-ac/c
                                      Sgt. Ivan O. Wick-arm.

Johnson, Albert G., Lt.   August 1943-April 29, 1944(POW)
(0-805057)   P-51B A9-V 42-106485 "Maggie's Drawers"

Kammerlohr, Morton A., Capt.   August 1943-August 1944; to States
(0-748688)   76 missions, 272 hours
                                      P-51B A9-I 43-7194 "Courser"

	P-51D A9-I 44-13706 "Courser II"
	S/Sgt. Dave H. Holbrook-c/c
	Sgt. Wilfred S. Hicks-ac/c
	Cpl. Roy B. Kerby-arm.
Kellogg, Merle M., Lt. (O-805067)	October 1943-August 1944; to States P-51B A9-X 43-6368 "It Sends Me" P-51B A9-X 43-6512 "It Sends Me" P-51D A9-N 44-14022 "Miss-Fire" S/Sgt. Howard E. Mosier-c/c Sgt. William T. Ahern-ac/c Cpl. Donald J. Van Sluyters-arm.
Kerns, Richard D., Lt. (O-748479)	August 1943-November 1943
Killingsworth, Thomas H., Lt. (O-692165)	May 1944-September 1944; to 9th WRS P-51B A9-L 43-6706
Lavin, Harry E., Jr., Lt. (O-810680)	May 1944-September 1944 P-51D A9- 44-13777
Lee, James W., Lt. (O-818395)	July 1944-September 1944
Lyman, Herbert F., Lt. (O-797359)	June 1944-June 17, 1944(KIA)
MacDonald, Robert H., Lt. (O-820239)	August 1944-August 1944; to 381st Ftr Sqn 2 missions
Maxwell, Paul R., Lt. (O-810538)	February 1944-April 22, 1944(POW) ex-365th Ftr Grp 11 missions, 41 hours
McCall, Evan M., Maj. (O-431134)	May 1943-July 1944; to 9th AF HdQts 36 missions P-51B A9-A 43-6516 "Fool's Paradise III" P-51D A9-A 44-13309 "Fool's Paradise IV"
McClung, Thomas S.L., Lt. (O-793008)	June 1944-September 1944; to 358th Ftr Grp and POW 3-1-45
McEachron, Gordon T., Capt. (O-748728)	August 1943-August 1944; to 354th Ftr Grp and POW 12-1-44 69 missions

	P-51B A9- 43-6330 "Beachcomber"
	P-51B A9- "Beachcomber II"
	P-51D A9- "Beachcomber III"

McKenna, James B., Lt.
(0-800543)

February 1944-April 11, 1944(MIA)
ex-365th Ftr Grp

McKinney, Walter A., Lt.
(0-748733)

August 1943-August 1944; to 354th Ftr Grp
111 missions total both groups
P-51B A9-N 43-7006 "Lil Bear"
S/Sgt. Erwin C. Derrick-c/c

Melancon, Alex J., Capt.
(0-666568)

March 1944-September 1944; to 354th Ftr Grp
ex-358th Ftr Grp
P-51C A9-M 42-103328
P-51D A9-M 44-13559

Messer, Henry B., Lt.
(0-810547)

February 1944-August 1944; to States
ex-365th Ftr Grp
P-51D A9- 44-13697

Metayer, Robert A., Lt.
(0-821526)

July 1944-September 1944

Molen, John E., Lt.
(0-810550)

February 1944-September 1944; to 358th Ftr Grp
and KIA 12-2-44; ex-365th Ftr Grp
84 missions total all groups
S/Sgt. Erwin C. Derrick-c/c
Sgt. Peter A. Bender-arm.

Moore, Charles L., Lt.
(0-810552)

February 1944-April 30, 1944(MIA-E)
ex-365th Ftr Grp

Morrison, Louis D., Capt.
(0-732314)

July 1944-August 1944; to States
ex-362nd Ftr Grp and 382nd Ftr Sqn
P-51D A9-R 44-13605
S/Sgt. Alvin J. Wolff-c/c
Sgt. Robert E. Watson-ac/c

Murphy, Eugene, Lt.
(0-820309)

July 1944-September 1944; to 364th Ftr Grp
and claimed 1.5 air kills

Nicholas, Ernest L., Jr., Lt.
(0-748755)

August 1943-June 19, 1944(KIA)

Nielsen, Myles R., Lt.
(0-820628)

August 1944-August 26, 1944(MIA)
4 missions

Owen, Arthur W., Jr., Lt.
(O-730592)

March 1944-April 29, 1944(MIA-E)

Oyler, John W., Lt.
(O-793016)

June 1944-July 4, 1944(MIA-E)

Pederson, Paul A., Lt.
(O-745494)

August 1943-November 1943; to 382nd Ftr Sqn

Ray, Donald W., Lt.
(O-804228)

August 1943-August 1944; to States
67 missions, 198 hours
P-51D A9- 44-13384 "Little Chico"
S/Sgt. Harold L. Burks-c/c
Sgt. Luther E. Lewis-arm.

Reddig, Charles R., Lt.
(O-748787)

August 1943-July 4, 1944(MIA-E)
49 missions
P-51B A9-F "Limited Service"

Reetzke, Lyle F., Lt.
(O-810565)

February 1944-June 25, 1944(POW); ex-
365th Ftr Grp

Reinholz, Albert W., Lt.
(O-748790)

August 1943-October 21, 1943(injured)

Robinson, Frank M., Lt.
(O-886089)

July 1944-September 1944
S/Sgt. Alvin J. Wolff-c/c
Sgt. Robert E. Watson-ac/c

Rolland, Paul O., Lt.
(O-766701)

July 1944-September 1944

Root, Merton E., Lt.
(O-744760)

August 1943-November 1943

Sample, Harry M., Capt.
(O-664061)

June 1944-July 1944; to HdQts

Sanford, Glenn F., Lt.
(O-744767)

August 1943-November 6, 1943(KIAc)

Schmidt, Paul W., Lt.
(O-820594)

August 1944-August 1944; to 381st Ftr Sqn
2 missions (none w/381st)

Schriber, Donald W., Lt.
(O-766720)

July 1944-September 1944; to 358th Ftr Grp
and claimed 1 kill

Schubert, William H., Lt.
(0-692204)

May 1944-September 1944; to 358th Ftr Grp
and claimed 1 kill
P-51B A9- 42-106645 "Schubert's Serenade"

Selby, Fred E., Lt.
(0-708764)

July 1944-September 1944; to 358th Ftr Grp
and KIA

Shantz, Edwin S., Lt.
(0-766728)

July 1944-September 1944; to 358th Ftr Grp
and KIA 10-15-44

Sharrock, John A., Jr., Lt.
(0-744774)

August 1943-April 22, 1944(MIA-E)
S/Sgt. Franklin Biere-c/c

Snyder, Earl L., Lt.
(0-744788)

August 1943-August 1944; to States

Sparer, Paul I., Lt.
(0-820616)

August 1944-August 1944; to 381st Ftr Sqn
4 missions (none w/381st)

Steiner, Walter H., Jr., Lt.
(0-743122)

May 1944-September 1944; ex-382nd Ftr Sqn
P-51B A9-E 43-6702
S/Sgt. Carl Monday-c/c
Sgt. John E. Braubach-ac/c
Cpl. Herbert H. Roeger-arm.

Stultz, Robert R., Lt.
(0-744794)

August 1943-November 1943

Tilson, Thomas J., Capt.
(0-744546)

August 1943-August 1944; to States
P-51B A9-Q 43-6804
P-51B A9-Q
P-51D A9-Q
Sgt. James M. Christensen-arm.

Tompkins, Norman L., Lt.
(0-711876)

August 1944-September 1944; to 354th Ftr Grp
4 missions

Turner, Bruce W., Lt.
(0-810603)

February 1944-June 20, 1944(POW); ex-365th
Ftr Grp
55 missions
P-51C A9-S 42-103335

Tyler, Ralph J., Lt.
(0-748848)

August 1943-August 1944; to States
P-51B A9-T "Honey Belle"
P-51B A9-T "Ballzout"

Ullo, Neill F., Lt.   August 1943-March 8, 1944(POW)
(0-744670)   4 missions
                                       P-51B A9-V 43-6932

Vance, Edwin E., Lt.   August 1943-June 11, 1944(KIA)
(0-744671)

Wharton, James N., Lt.   May 1944-September 1944; to 358th Ftr Grp
(0-692240)

Williams, Burl R., Capt.   November 1943-July 27, 1944(POW)
(0-804262)   P-51B A9- "Oklahoma Kid"
                                       P-51B A9- "Oklahoma Kid II"
                                       P-51D A9- 44-13310 "Oklahoma Kid III"

Wisdom. Rolland L., Lt.   August 1944-September 1944; to 362nd Ftr Grp
(0-1171845)   0 missions

Wisner, Raymond R., Capt.   May 1944-September 1944; ex-HdQts and
(0-745559)   381st Ftr Sqn; later to 358th Ftr Grp
                                       P-51B A9- 42-106765 "Bless Bess"

381st Fighter Squadron

Adair, Asa A., Capt.   Flew training missions on February 24, 28, and 29
(0-659624)   and March 3, plus a combat flight on February 25;
                                       possibly a Wing officer assigned to help transition
                                       to P-51's(?) Later with 50th Ftr Grp

Baer, Harold R., Lt.   July 1944-September 1944; to 362nd Ftr Grp
(0-801445)   28 missions

Baird, John J., Lt.   June 1944-August 1944; to 354th Ftr Grp
(0-730332)   35 missions (381st only); ex-354th Ftr Grp

Benbenek, Daren L., Lt.   August 1943-March 20, 1944(MIA)
(0-748527)   9 missions
                                       P-51B B3- 43-6434

Berglind, Elmo H., Lt.   August 1943-March 18, 1944(MIA-E)
(0-748730)   9 missions
                                       P-51B B3- 43-6711

Billings, Archie E., Lt.   August 1944-September 1944; to 362nd Ftr Grp
(0-711921)   and MIA 2-13-45
                                       5 missions

Boland, Jeremiah M., Capt.
(0-748537)

August 1943-August 1944; to States
77 missions
P-51B B3- 43-6647
P-51B B3- 42-106822
P-51D B3- 44-13590 "Frankie Boy"
Sgt. Donald A. Baird-arm.

Byerly, Melvin I., F/O
(T-124879)

August 1944-September 1944; to 406th Ftr Grp
7 missions

Carter, James R., Jr., Capt.
(0-749523)

August 1943-August 1944; to States
67 missions (plus 6 in Italy on D/S)
P-51B B3- 43-6361
P-51C B3- 42-103591
P-51D B3- 44-13548 "Skywolf"
Sgt. James E. Fitzgerald-arm.

Clark, Paul F., Lt.
(0-816473)

June 1944-June 24, 1944(MIA-E)
10 missions

Culberson, Dave H., Maj.
(0-431126)

April 1943-July 26, 1944(KIAc); ex-HdQts
58 missions
P-51B B3-A 43-6458 "Huntin' Trouble"
P-51D B3-A 44-13327 "Huntin' Trouble II"
S/Sgt. Weldon A. Lee-c/c
Cpl. Peter H. Bedrosian-arm.

Dalglish, James B., Capt.
(0-886127)

March 1944-June 1944; ex-354th Ftr Grp and
back to 354th Ftr Grp
42 missions (381st only)
P-51B B3-D 42-106834
P-51D B3-D 44-13396

Davis, Clifford H., Lt.
(0-886287)

March 1944-June 1944; to 354th Ftr Grp
and claimed 0.5 air kills
33 missions
P-51B B3- 43-6949 "Lady Joan III"
S/Sgt. Milton L. Sims-c/c
Sgt. Robert D. Poole-ac/c
Sgt. Wren J. Dillard-arm.

di Zerega, Augustus, Lt.
(0-814666)

June 1944-August 28, 1944(MIA-E)
28 missions

Doerr, George R., Capt.
(0-730405)

July 1943-April 22, 1944(POW)
10 missions
P-51B B3-W 43-6426 "Pegasus"

Doran, Keith W., Lt.
(0-818347)

June 1944-July 4, 1944(KIA)
3 missions

Early, John E., Lt.
(0-678000)

June 1944-September 1944; to 373rd Ftr Grp
36 missions
P-51B B3- 42-106743

Freyermuth, Russell D., Lt.
(0-659806)

May 1944-June 1944; to States
28 missions
P-51B B3- 42-106888

Gallagher, Charles L., Lt.
(0-805026)

August 1943-August 1944; to States
71 missions
P-51B B3-S 43-6691 "Squirrel"
P-51B B3-S 42-106453 "Squirrel"
P-51D B3-S 44-13340 "Squirrel"
S/Sgt. Stephen J. DeMarco-c/c
Sgt. Delton F. Kuntz-ac/c
Sgt. John C. Roussell-arm.

Gervan, John, Lt.
(0-805029)

April 1944-July 4, 1944(KIA); formerly flew
in Iceland
52 missions
P-51B B3- 42-106734

Gough, C.H., F/O
(T-?????)

Flew a training mission on April 10 but never
was listed on the flight logs after that.

Gustafson, Victor G., Lt.
(0-748633)

August 1943-March 4, 1944(KIA)
2 missions

Henry, Patrick H., Lt.
(0-694240)

March 1944-August 1944
62 missions
P-51B B3-H 43-6954

Heyne, Richard L., Lt.
(0-712005)

August 1944-September 1944; to 362nd Ftr Grp
and MIA 10-28-44
6 missions

Hirsch, Lee H., Jr., Lt.
(0-748649)

August 1943-November 1943

Howard, Harold R., Lt.
(0-748730)

August 1943-November 1943

Howell, Harry R., Lt.
(0-748654)

August 1943-April 12, 1944(POW)
13 missions
P-51B B3- 43-6522

Hudgens, Harry R., Lt.
(0-737109)

July 1944-August 1944; to 358th Ftr Grp
29 missions

Jacobs, Keith L., Lt.
(0-748663)

August 1943-April 1944; transferred
8 missions
P-51B B3- 43-6822

Jacobson, Norman H., Lt.
(0-694163)

March 1944-August 1944; to States
71 missions, 190 hours
P-51B B3-F 43-6505 "Sugar Foot"
P-51B B3-F 42-106731 "Sugar Foot II"
P-51D B3-V 44-13644 "Sugar Foot III"
S/Sgt. Dominic F. Morazzo-c/c
Sgt. William Decho-ac/c
Sgt. Bernard J. Quinn-arm.

Johnson, Richard O., Lt.
(0-704681)

July 1944-September 1944; to 358th Ftr Grp
and claimed 1 kill
31 missions

Johnson, Virgil T., Lt.
(0-687427)

January 1944-June 17, 1944(KIA)
35 missions
P-51B B3- 43-6657 "Little Jinnie"
P-51B B3- 42-106729
S/Sgt. D.L. Jackson-c/c
Sgt. Martin V. Tilley-ac/c
Cpl. Joe F. Shull-arm.

Jones, Warren A., Lt.
(0-766547)

July 1944-September 1944; to 358th Ftr Grp
and KIA
32 missions

Kemmerer, Edward W., Lt.
(0-694166)

March 1944-June 17, 1944(POW)
29 missions
P-51B B3- "Damn Yankee"

Kennedy, Robert E., Lt.
(0-694253)

March 1944-May 24, 1944(KIA)
24 missions

Kiamy, Philip J., Lt.
(0-749536)

August 1943-November 1943

Kiesig, Carl L., Lt.   August 1943-October 3, 1943(KIAc)
(0-748679)

Kilfoyle, Thomas T., Jr., Lt .   July 1944-September 1944; to 358th Ftr Grp
(0-766557)   and KIA 1-19-45
                                        23 missions

Kilpatrick, Robert L., Lt.   July 1944-September 1944; to 358th Ftr Grp
(0-766558)   30 missions

Knuppel, Harry D., Capt.   August 1943-August 1944; to States
(0-748682)   54 missions (plus 8 in Italy on D/S)
                                        P-51B B3-U 43-6744
                                        P-51B B3-U 43-7108
                                        P-51D B3-U 44-13373 "Voodoo"
                                        S/Sgt. William P. Turner-c/c
                                        Sgt. Wilton T. Turner-ac/c
                                        Sgt. Wilbur R. Lundy-arm.

Krehbiel, Burman C., Lt.   August 1943-November 1943
(0-748686)

Lasko, Charles W., Capt.   July 1944-August 1944; ex-354th Ftr Grp
(0-730540)   19 missions
                                        P-51D B3- 44-13622 "Buster"
                                        Cpl. Peter H. Bedrosian-arm.

Leety, Robert M., Lt.   July 1944-September 1944; to 358th Ftr Grp
(0-704689)   and KIA 3-15-45
                                        33 missions

Lowers, Daniel E., Lt.   June 1944-September 1944; to 358th Ftr Grp
(0-821741)   38 missions
                                        P-51B B3-B 43-6797 "Snark"
                                        S/Sgt. Wallace T. Goodhue-c/c

Lucas, Richard P., Lt.   February 1944-May 24, 1944(POW)
(0-810529)   ex-365th Ftr Grp
                                        38 missions
                                        P-51B B3- 42-106877 "Suzabelle"

MacDonald, Robert H., Lt.   August 1944-September 1944; ex-380th Ftr Sqn
(0-820239)   and stayed on w/363rd Tac Recon Grp
                                        P-51B B3-L
                                        S/Sgt. Anton J. Cocek-c/c

Mahler, Henry D., Lt.
(0-748711)

August 1943-October 1943; later to CBI with 459th Ftr Sqn and claimed 3 kills.

Marks, Howard H., Lt.
(0-708727)

July 1944-September 1944
20 missions

Marlette, Jack A., Lt.
(0-708728)

July 1944-September 1944; to 362nd Ftr Grp
18 missions

McCowan, Fuller, Lt.
(0-685323)

July 1944-August 9, 1944(MIA-E)
25 missions

McGrath, Gordon J., Lt.
(0-708721)

August 1944-September 1944; to 362nd Ftr Grp and KIA 1-15-45
10 missions

McRoberts, Samuel L., Jr., Lt.
(0-805086)

October 1943-April 15, 1944(KIA)
13 missions
P-51B B3- 43-6752

Miller, Ward F., Lt.
(0-745642)

August 1943-April 22, 1944(POW)
10 missions
P-51B B3- 43-6769 "Flipped Lid"

Mimler, Arthur M., Lt.
(0-805094)

October 1943-June 14, 1944(POW)
45 missions
P-51B B3-C 43-6446 "Ginny/Ellie"

Monyelle, Louis A., Lt.
(0-748498)

August 1943-November 18, 1943(injured)

Morgan, Johnson T., Lt.
(0-792622)

August 1944-September 1944; to 405th Ftr Grp and claimed 1 kill
3 missions

Morgan, William R., Lt.
(0-792623)

August 1944-September 1944; to 405th Ftr Grp and claimed 1 kill
3 missions

Morton, Duncan M., Lt.
(0-708742)

August 1944-September 1944; to 362nd Ftr Grp
7 missions

Moyer, Louis, Lt.
(0-748744)

August 1943-March 4, 1944(KIA)
4 missions
P-51B B3- 43-6951

Munder, Fred A., Jr., Capt.
(0-744739)

August 1943-August 1944; to States
62 missions, 208:40 hours
P-51B B3-Y 43-6715 "Skyczar"
P-51D B3-Y 44-14059 "Skyczar"
S/Sgt. John White-c/c
Sgt. Ken L. Prior-ac/c

Myers, Edward M., Lt.
(0-686006)

June 1944-July 11, 1944(MIA-E); to 362nd Ftr Grp
and claimed 1 kill
7 missions

Neal, Charles A., Lt.
(0-744740)

August 1943-November 1943

Newman, James G., Lt.
(0-708749)

July 1944-September 1944; to 362nd Ftr Grp
and claimed 1 kill before KIA 11-20-44
25 missions

Owings, Theodore D., Lt.
(0-748766)

August 1943-March 4, 1944(KIA)
2 missions

Pate, James A., Lt.
(0-44225)

May 1944-August 1944; to 496th Ftr Trg Grp
ex-354th Ftr Grp
24 missions

Plunkett, Meredith W., Lt.
(0-?????)

August 1943-November 1943

Polley, Leonard H., Lt.
(0-748782)

August 1943-March 4, 1944(KIA)
1 mission

Pressnall, Hugo E., Lt.
(0-667756)

June 1944-August 1944; to 354th Ftr Grp
48 missions
P-51B B3-I 43-6568 "Tear Azz"
P-51D B3-I 44-13672 "Sword of the Spirit"
S/Sgt. Eugene A. Renneker-c/c(P-51B)
Sgt. John Kelly-arm.(P-51B)
S/Sgt. Michael Fekete-c/c(P-51D)
Sgt. Nicholas Marinelli-ac/c(P-51D)
Sgt. Carroll C. Andrinks-arm.(P-51D)

Recagno, George L., Capt.
(0-748786)

August 1943-August 1944; to 354th Ftr Grp and
claimed 0.5 air kills
66 missions, 203:55 hours
P-51B B3-V 43-6568 "Lee II"
P-51B B3-V 42-106705 "Lee II"

P-51D B3-V 44-13644 "Lee II"
S/Sgt. Dominic F. Morazzo-c/c
Sgt. Bernard J. Quinn-arm.

Reinhart, Albert J., Lt.
(0-810567)

February 1944-August 8, 1944(injured); ex-365th
Ftr Grp and later to 36th Ftr Grp claiming 2 kills.
56 missions
P-51B B3- 43-6522 "Mr. X"
P-51B B3- 43-6744

Richardson, James G., Lt.
(0-754198)

June 1944-September 1944; to 362nd Ftr Grp and
KIA 1-14-45
47 missions

Ringgenberg, Harold W., Lt.
(0-748796)

August 1943-July 1944; to 9th Bomber Command
29 missions
P-51B B3- 43-6994
P-51B B3- 42-106616

Schmidt, Paul W., Lt.
(0-820594)

August 1944-September 1944; ex-380th Ftr Sqn
0 missions

Schmidt, William R., Lt.
(0-745522)

August 1943-May 24, 1944(KIA)
30 missions
P-51B B3-I 43-6568
S/Sgt. Eugene A. Renneker-c/c
Sgt. John Kelly-arm.

Scott, Gerald B., F/O
(T-61264)

February 1944-August 1944; ex-365th Ftr Grp
77 missions
P-51B B3-M 42-106772 "Lady Patricia"

Scott, Harold E., Lt.
(0-748812)

August 1943-July 4, 1944(KIA)
46 missions
P-51C B3-H 42-103289
P-51B B3-H 43-6954

Shea, Charles E., Lt.
(0-810580)

February 1944-August 1944; ex-365th Ftr Grp
71 missions
P-51B B3-B 43-6797 "Snark"
P-51D B3-D 44-13396 "One Long Hop"
S/Sgt. Harold Hansen-c/c
Sgt. Elton L. Ritchey-ac/c
Sgt. Charles W. Moyle-arm.

Smith, Charles H., Lt.
(O-748820)

August 1943-May 24, 1944(POW)
24 missions
P-51B B3-D 43-6463 "Dee"
P-51B B3-D 42-106731 "Dee"
S/Sgt. Niels F. Peterson-c/c

Smutz, Leonard D., Lt.
(O-810587)

February 1944-June 1944 (injured April 27)
ex-365th Ftr Grp
12 missions
P-51B B3- 43-6953

Sparer, Paul I., Lt.
(O-820616)

August 1944-September 1944; ex-380th Ftr Sqn
stayed w/363rd Tac Rec Grp and claimed 1 kill
0 missions

Spencer, Robert E., Lt.
(O-804244)

August 1943-March 20, 1944(KIA)
4 missions

Steinke, William W., Lt.
(O-749552)

August 1943-April 9, 1944(KIA)
11 missions
P-51B B3-E 42-106466 "Sand and Sage"

Stuart, Charles F., Lt.
(O-810593)

February 1944-August 1944; to States; ex-365th
Ftr Grp
67 missions
P-51B B3-E 43-24752 "Stinky"

Sullivan, Burr H., Lt.
(O-748834)

August 1943-March 4, 1944(KIA)
3 missions

Tait, Alexander H., Lt.
(O-793028)

June 1944-August 1944; to 371st Ftr Grp and
claimed 1 kill
42 missions
P-51B B3-C 43-6446

Thoresz, Joseph J., Lt.
(O-810598)

February 1944-August 1944; to States; ex-365th
Ftr Grp
62 missions, 204 hours
P-51B B3-Z 42-106740 "Honk Honk"
S/Sgt. James F. Evans-c/c
Sgt. Riley H. Courreges-ac/c
Cpl. Jess Greer-arm.

Trumbower, Fred W., Lt.
(O-737499)

June 1944-September 1944; to 371st Ftr Grp
32 missions
P-51B B3- 43-6458 "Killer"
Sgt. Harold H. Hass-arm.

Tucker, Davis R., Lt.
(0-810600)

February 1944-August 1944; to States; ex-365th
Ftr Grp
75 missions
P-51B B3-G 43-6979 "Tarheel Special"
S/Sgt. Anton J. Cocek-c/c
Sgt. Irvin Meinken-ac/c

Tyree, Newman E., Lt.
(0-812509)

March 1944-March 25, 1944(KIAc)
2 missions

Vesely, Edward J., Lt.
(0-812907)

March 1944-June 15, 1944(MIA-E)
30 missions
P-51B B3-R 43-7138 "Rex"
Cpl. Robert A. Lewis-arm.

Webb, William A., Jr., Lt.
(0-810607)

February 1944-July 1944; to 1st General Hospital
(WIA May 24); ex-365th Ftr Grp
26 missions
P-51B B3- 43-6659
P-51B B3- 43-7056

Wheeler, Lloyd E., Lt.
(0-667764)

June 1944-August 1944; to 371st Ftr Grp
36 missions

White, James W., Lt.
(0-807652)

June 1944-June 19, 1944(KIA)
5 missions

Whited, Walter C., Lt.
(0-701214)

June 1944-August 1944; to 362nd Ftr Grp and
claimed 1 air & 2 grd kills
27 missions

Wieczorek, Henry, Lt.
(0-701215)

June 1944-September 1944; to 371st Ftr Grp
and MIA 1-22-45
30 missions

Williams, Ben D., Lt.
(0-812523)

March 1944-August 1944
71 missions
P-51B B3- 42-106734
S/Sgt. Gerald J. Miller-c/c
Sgt. Milton A. Mahaffey-ac/c
Cpl. Lester Salzwedel-arm.

Wisner, Raymond R., Lt.
(0-745559)

August 1943-November 1943; to HdQts

Wood, Paul W., Jr., Lt.
(0-812525)

March 1944-June 29, 1944(MIA)
40 missions
P-51B B3- 43-6514

Yochim, Walter H., T/Sgt.
(T-10601574)

May 1944-June 17, 1944(KIA); ex-382nd Ftr Sqn

382nd Fighter Squadron

Abramovitz, Marvin, Lt.
(0-711827)

August 1944-September 1944; to 371st Ftr Grp
4 missions

Aldrich, Lester F., Lt.
(0-802301)

August 1943-March 4, 1944(KIA)
P-51B C3-O
S/Sgt. Richard A. O'Connor-c/c

Archilla, Eliel, Lt.
(0-711902)

August 1944-September 1944; to 371st Ftr Grp

Asbury, Richard W., Lt.
(0-801346)

August 1943-August 1944; to 354th Ftr Grp
and claimed 3.5 air kills
62 missions, 200 hours
P-51B C3-R 43-6761 "Queenie"
P-51B C3-R 42-106619 "Queenie II"
S/Sgt. George P. Linkinhoker-c/c
Cpl. Jack W. Larson-arm.

Bailey, Harry L., Lt.
(0-763461)

June 1944-August 1944; to 371st Ftr Grp and
claimed 1 kill

Barlow, James E., Lt.
(0-748519)

August 1943-November 1943; to 380th Ftr Sqn

Bearden, Aaron L., Lt.
(0-748524)

August 1943-November 1943; later to CBI
w/459th Ftr Sqn and claimed 5 air kills before
KIA 9-3-44

Bingham, Bayard B., Lt.
(0-748532)

August 1943-August 1944; to States
P-51B C3-K 43-6377 "Quitcher' Kickin"
S/Sgt. Robert W. Yates-c/c
Sgt. Stanley L. Gardner-ac/c
Cpl. H. Kines-arm.

Boatright, Donald L., Lt.
(0-749521)

August 1943-June 1944; taken off operations
April 11 due to wounds.
P-51B C3-H 43-6905 "Destiny's Tot"

Bortle, Walter H., Lt.   June 1944-September 1944
(0-667641)

Brink, James N., Capt.   August 1943-August 1944; to States
(0-740357)   77 missions, 230 hours
                                P-51B C3-P "Roscoe II"
                                P-51D C3-P 44-13554 "Roscoe II"
                                S/Sgt. Kenneth K. Thach-c/c
                                Cpl. Edward Pollack-arm.

Brooks, George J., Lt.   July 1944-August 13, 1944(MIA-E); later to
(0-706347)   9th WRS
                                5 missions, 11 hours

Brown, John R., Jr., Capt.   March 1944-August 8, 1944(MIA-E)
(0-795905)   ex-362nd Ftr Grp and later 414th Ftr Grp, PTO
                                61 missions
                                P-51B C3-D 42-106647 "Big Mac Junior"
                                S/Sgt. William A. Prosneick-c/c
                                Cpl. Jerome Schwartz-arm.

Bullard, William E., Lt.   February 1944-July 18, 1944(POW)
(0-748553)   38 missions, 150 hours
                                P-51B C3-X 43-6830 "El Malo Hombre"
                                S/Sgt. Morris S. Easterly-c/c
                                Sgt. Fred W. Nelson-ac/c
                                Cpl. James E. Huffman-arm.

Buskey, Douglas H., Capt.   July 1944-September 1944; ex-bomber pilot
(0-432309)   (30 missions, 182:50 hours)

Cahill, Edward F., Lt.   August 1943-April 15, 1944(KIA)
(0-677025)

Camden, Donald K., Lt.   August 1943-October 21, 1943(KIAc)
(0-748560)

Campbell, Edward B., Lt.   August 1943-November 1943
(0-748561)

Clark, James H., Lt.   August 1943-August 1944; to States
(0-749526)   65 missions, 205 hours
                                P-51B C3-G "The Mighty Midget"
                                S/Sgt. Emanuel Ehlenberger-c/c
                                Cpl. Peter Sikula-ac/c
                                Cpl. Tom H. Strzynski-arm.

Coble, Robert P., Lt.
(0-748575)

August 1943-April 15, 1944(POW)
Lost while on D/S in Italy

Collins, Willie D., F/O
(T-1436)

August 1943-March 4, 1944(KIA)

Deeds, Fred B., Lt.
(0-748589)

August 1943-May 1944; to 354th Ftr Grp and
claimed 1.5 kills

Eaton, Kenneth W., Lt.
(0-826642)

August 1944-September 1944; to 405th Ftr Grp

Edwards, Joseph R., Lt.
(0-748605)

August 1943-March 4, 1944(KIA)

Fogelquist, Elmer W., F/O
(T-124077)

July 1944-September 1944; to 9th WRS

Frye, Donald E., Lt.
(0-442049)

June 1944-September 1944; to 373rd Ftr Grp
ex-RAF and 354th Ftr Grp

Gilbert, Donald M., F/O
(T-2684)

August 1944-September 1944

Hamilton, Willard V., Lt.
(0-532974)

June 1944-June 21, 1944(POW)

Hardwick, Earvel D., Lt.
(0-748658)

August 1943-November 1943

Hare, Clifford W., T/Sgt.
(T-????)

January 1944-April 15, 1944(KIA)

Hayes, Thomas L., Lt.
(0-403857)

March 1943-April 1943; to 357th Ftr Grp and
later to ETO claiming 8.5 air kills. ex-PTO vet

Heberlein, Robert M., Lt.
(0-748645)

August 1943-August 1944; to States
72 missions
P-51B C3- "Pudge"

Hopkins, Stanhope F., Lt.
(0-712012)

August 1944-September 1944; to 371st Ftr Grp

Hudson, Dell P., Lt.
(0-748657)

August 1943-November 1943; to HdQts
July 1944-August 13, 1944(KIA)
S/Sgt. Joe E. McDonald-c/c

Jabara, James, Lt.
(0-694162)

March 1944-August 1944; to 355th Ftr Grp
and claimed 5.5 grd kills
S/Sgt. Charles C. Dartt-c/c
Sgt. Peter L. Eglinton-ac/c
Cpl. John L. Williamson-arm.

Jones, Halvor K., Lt.
(0-1995982)

June 1944-September 1944; to 373rd Ftr Grp
and claimed 0.5 air kills

King, David L., Lt.
(0-674045)

June 1944-September 1944; to 373rd Ftr Grp
and claimed 4 air kills
P-51D C3- 44-13408

King, Wallace N., Lt.
(0-714440)

August 1944-September 1944; to 406th Ftr Grp
(flew 75 missions and POW April 1945)
0 missions w/363rd

Kozaczka, Felix, Lt.
(0-694254)

March 1944-August 1944; to 354th Ftr Grp
and claimed 2 air kills
70 missions
P-51B C3- 42-106887

Kuhl, Lawrence A., Lt.
(0-714443)

August 1944-September 1944; to 405th Ftr Grp

Kunz, Robert D., Lt.
(0-748689)

August 1943-June 1944; to HdQts
P-51B C3- 43-7016 "Frisco Kid"
P-51D C3- "El Don"

Ladas, Anthony, Lt.
(0-810522)

February 1944-May 28, 1944(KIA); ex-365th
Ftr Grp

Lamar, Robert M., Lt.
(0-678066)

June 1944-September 1944; to 354th Ftr Grp
P-51B C3-X 42-106621
S/Sgt. Morris S. Easterly-c/c
Sgt. Fred W. Nelson-ac/c
Cpl. James E. Huffman-arm.
Cpl. Allan L. Driver-arm.

Lewis, Donald M., Lt.
(0-748699)

September 1943-April 5, 1944(MIA-E)

Littlefield, Warren C., Lt.
(0-793942)

June 1944-September 1944; to 354th Ftr Grp
and claimed 1 air kill

Loesch, Charles M., F/O
(T-61813)

July 1944-September 1944; to 405th Ftr Grp
and claimed 1 air kill before KIA 12-30-44

McGee, Robert B., Capt.
(0-748730)

August 1943-August 1944; to States
P-51B C3-A 42-106486 "Virginia"
P-51D C3-A "Virginia"
S/Sgt. Kenard J. Slocum-c/c

McGee, Wilbur E., Lt.
(0-748731)

August 1943-March 4, 1944(KIA)

McWherter, Robert C., Maj.
(0-421123)

May 1943-August 1944; to States
ex-17th Pur Sqn, PTO with 1 air kill
P-51B C3-M 43-6438 "Hoo Flung Dung"
P-51D C3-M 44-13380 "Hoo Flung Dung"
S/Sgt. Alfred W. Swift-c/c
Sgt. William L. Hughes-arm.

Morrison, Louis D., Capt.
(0-732314)

March 1944-July 1944; to 380th Ftr Sqn
ex-362nd Ftr Grp
P-51B C3- "Toni Girl"

Odell, Elmer W., Lt.
(0-810555)

February 1944-August 1944; to States
ex-365th Ftr Grp
67 missions, 172 hours
P-51B C3-V "El's Belle Ginny"
S/Sgt. Richard A. Quinn-c/c
Sgt. Robert C. Heine-arm.

Ott, Norman E., Lt.
(0-820316)

July 1944-September 1944; to 9th WRS
16 missions

Palmer, Carleton E., Lt.
(0-701798)

June 1944-September 1944; to 9th WRS and
KIAc 4-45

Panner, Edward J., Lt.
(0-708755)

August 1944-September 1944; stayed with
363rd Tac Recon Grp

Parker, George F., Lt.
(0-810557)

February 1944-March 30, 1944(KIAc); ex-
365th Ftr Grp

Pavelich, Frank J., Lt.
(0-759069)

May 1944-August 1944; to 354th Ftr Grp and
claimed 1 air kill before KIA 9-28-44

Pawlak, Edward T., Lt.
(0-748771)

August 1943-September 1944; to 405th Ftr Grp
54 missions (20 more w/405th)
P-51B C3-W 43-24837
P-51C C3-W 43-25045 "My Pal Snookie"
S/Sgt. John W. Pacey-c/c
Cpl. Joe F. Caterinechia-arm.

Pederson, Paul A., Lt.
(0-745494)

November 1943-February 2, 1944(KIAc)
ex-380th Ftr Sqn

Peterson, George W., Lt.
(0-748766)

August 1943-November 1943; later to ETO
w/55th Ftr Grp and POW 6-16-44

Pollard, Benjamin A., Lt.
(0-745499)

October 1943-April 9, 1944(KIA)

Proctor, Robert E., Lt.
(0-810563)

February 1944-September 1944; ex-365th Ftr Grp
52 missions, 201 hours
P-51B C3-C 43-6360 "de-RUMBLE-izer"
P-51B C3-C 42-106899
P-51B C3-C 42-106737

Reeves, Gordon E., Lt.
(0-758852)

May 1944-September 1944; to 354th Ftr Grp
Sgt. Jesse R. Burk-c/c
Sgt. Joe J. Petrusick-ac/c
Cpl. Lloyd H. Phinney-arm.

Rice, Chester H., Lt.
(0-820326)

June 1944-August 13, 1944(KIA)

Robertson, John, Capt.
(0-885997)

March 1944-August 1944; to 354th Ftr Grp
ex-RAF and 67th Tac Recon Grp
86 missions, 300 hours
P-51B C3- 43-6952 "Donna Mae"
P-51D C3- "Donna Mae"
S/Sgt. Charles C. Dartt-c/c
Cpl. John L. Williamson-arm.

Rook, Dale H., Lt.
(0-681706)

August 1943-May 30, 1944(KIA)
P-51B C3- "Pied Piper"

Santarlasci, Joseph H., Lt.
(0-810573)

February 1944-August 1944; to States
ex-365th Ftr Grp
57 missions
P-51B C3-N 43-6859 "Rose O'Day"
S/Sgt. Roy L. Williams-c/c

Schillereff, Raymond E., Lt.
(0-748809)

August 1943-August 1944; to States
P-51B C3-L "Princess Marge"
S/Sgt. Gordon E. Garner-c/c

Schmidt, John W., Capt.
(0-748810)

August 1943-August 1944; to States
P-51B C3-O 43-6435
S/Sgt. Richard A. O'Connor-c/c

Shiff, Charles H., Jr., Lt.
(0-812499)

March 1944-August 1944; to States
83 missions, 206:15 hours
P-51B C3-V 43-6713 "Marion"
S/Sgt. Joseph E. McDonald-c/c
Sgt. John W. Pacey-ac/c
Cpl. John J. Mahoney-arm.

Sickling, Herbert W., Lt.
(0-671781)

June 1944-August 1944; to 406th Ftr Grp
and claimed 1 air kill; ex-354th Ftr Grp

Smith, John I., Lt.
(0-711866)

August 1944-September 1944; to 406th Ftr Grp

Stearns, Carroll A., Lt.
(0-812505)

March 1944-May 30, 1944(MIA-E)
25 missions

Steiner, Walter H., Jr., Lt.
(0-743122)

August 1943-May 1944; to 380th Ftr Sqn

Stricker, John R., Lt.
(0-810591)

February 1944-August 1944; to States
ex-365th Ftr Grp
P-51C C3-B 42-103613 "Green Hornet"
S/Sgt. John L. Ross-c/c
Sgt. Harold J. Roberts-ac/c

Sullivan, Stewart P., Lt.
(0-754228)

February 1944-March 21, 1944(KIAc)
ex-365th Ftr Grp

Sykes, Ross S., Lt.
(0-811544)

March 1944-May 1, 1944(KIA)

Theil, John H., Lt.
(0-748840)

August 1943-March 4, 1944(KIA)

Thompson, Marvin A., Lt.
(0-744799)

August 1943-June 25, 1944(MIA-E)
P-51B C3-J 43-6542 "Little Chris II"
S/Sgt. Robert G. Ross-c/c
Cpl. Joe M. Upperman-arm.

Torbet, Robert P., Lt.
(0-714528)

August 1944-September 1944; to 405th Ftr Grp

Underwood, Bedford R., Lt.
(0-666568)

July 1944-September 1944; to 406th Ftr Grp
and claimed 1 air kill

Wackerbarth, Kenneth D., Lt.
(0-713048)

August 1944-September 1944; to 406th Ftr Grp
(flew 3 missions and POW September 1944)
0 missions w/363rd

Warden, Harry L., Lt.
(0-748864)

August 1943-November 1943

Warner, Jack A., Lt.
(0-805714)

February 1944-August 1944; to 354th Ftr Grp
and claimed 5 air kills; ex-365th Ftr Grp
69 missions, 199:55 hours
P-51B C3-T 43-6447 "Lady June"
S/Sgt. Homer P. Tunger-c/c
Sgt. Mike W. Scirocco-ac/c

Watkins, Edwin G., Lt.
(0-812517)

March 1944-March 21, 1944(KIAc)

Watson, James E., Lt.
(0-748855)

August 1943-March 4, 1944(KIA)

Webster, Lee E., Lt.
(0-812519)

March 1944-August 1944; to States
73 missions, 282 hours
P-51B C3- "Gracious"

Wenner, John A., Lt.
(0-810609)

February 1944-April 8, 1944(MIA)
ex-365th Ftr Grp

Williams, Donald E., Lt.
(0-671821)

June 1944-September 1944; ex-354th Ftr Grp

Wilson, Curry P., Lt.
(0-1294757)

May 1944-May 28, 1944(POW)
15 missions
Cpl. Adrian Zielke-arm.

Winham, Harrie A., Lt.
(0-423389)

June 1944-June 25, 1944(MIA); ex-354th Ftr Grp

Yochim, Walter H., T/Sgt.
(T-10601574)

January 1944-May 1944; to 381st Ftr Sqn

Yothers, Ralph W., Lt.
(0-797761)

July 1944-September 1944; to 405th Ftr Grp
and claimed 1 air kill

Appendix 8
Aircraft Markings

While training in the United States, the 363rd Fighter Group was equipped with Bell P-39 AIRACOBRAS. These were all finished in the standard Army Air Force scheme of olive drab upper and neutral gray lower surfaces. The majority of the aircraft had white spinners and, in some cases, cowl bands. Shortly after training started, however, the 382nd Fighter Squadron acquired yellow noses. It is currently not known if the other two squadrons received any color markings on their ships or not. While at Santa Rosa, aircraft numbers were allotted to the squadrons, with the runs being: 10-39 for the 380th, 40-69 for the 381st, and 70-99 for the 382nd.

After the squadrons split up in October of 1943, the P-39's received a new run of numbers: 110-139 for the 380th, 140-169 for the 381st, and 170-199 for the 382nd. As before, these were applied to the forward nose area in white. The author has seen very few P-39 photos of the 363rd, however, the ones viewed tend to support the above series. For example, at Santa Rosa, the 380th had P-39's with the numbers 11 and 23, while at Oakland, the 381st had a number 163 and the 382nd had numbers 199 (James Brink's "Roscoe II" and formerly number 99 at Santa Rosa) and 196. The 380th had numbers 110 (Evan McCall's "Fool's Paradise II"), 125 (Walter McKinney's ship), 121, 130, 133, and 137.

Initial aircraft for the 363rd upon arrival in England were P-51B Mustangs. These planes were finished in the same scheme of olive drab upper and neutral gray lower surfaces with white Theater Bands as follows: a 12 inch band horizontally around the fin and rudder (these began to be removed in late March), a 15 inch band around each horizontal stabilizer, a 15 inch band around each wing about a foot outward of the wing-root, and all white spinners and 12 inch cowl band. Starting in March, natural metal finish P-51B's and C's were taken on and the Theater Bands and spinners were now in black.

Each squadron was issued radio code letters, placed in 24 inch high white (black on natural metal finish ships) letters on the fuselage, forward of the national insignia. These were: A9 for the 380th, B3 for the 381st, and C3 for the 382nd. In addition, each plane had an individual aircraft letter placed aft of the national insignia. Where two planes had the same letter, a bar was placed below the letter on one of the planes, i.e. A̲.

Starting on June 5, all Mustangs received an application of the so-called "Invasion Stripes", 18 inch wide white and black bands (three white, two black) around the tops and bottoms of the wings and around the fuselage behind the cockpit. By July these stripes were beginning to be removed from the upper surfaces of the wings and fuselage but the lower stripes remained. In some instances the stripes were removed down to the bare metal while in other cases they were simply overpainted with dark or olive green, resulting in a number of semi-camouflaged P-51's.

After the move to France, the P-51s began to sport colored spinners and cowl bands to identify the squadrons. The colors were blue for the 380th, red for the 381st, and yellow for the 382nd. In some instances the cowl band was backed by a thin black line and some 382nd planes kept the black cowl band with the yellow spinner.

Other markings carried were of a personal nature-names and drawings on the nose or under the cockpit area, pilot and groundcrew names, mission markers, victory markings (Lt. Jacobs of the 381st even had his balloon "kill" recorded), etc. Lastly, at least three 382nd P-51B's, J.R. Brown's "Big Mac Junior", R.B. McGee's "Virginia", and J.H. Clark's "The Mighty Midget", sported colorful sharkmouths. (As did McGee's later P-51D, also named "Virginia"). All three of these pilots were assigned to "A" Flight and as far as can be determined, no other 382nd planes were so marked.

Appendix 9
Representative Aircraft

Abbreviations: MIA (Missing in action), MIAc (destroyed in accident, both fatal and non-fatal), B/O (bailed out over Allied territory), CL (crash-landed and repaired), DCL (destroyed in a crash landing), ASR (pilot was rescued from Channel)

P-51C-1-NT

42-102992 C3-I		MIAc 3-21-44 *Sullivan*
42-102994 B3-		MIAc 3-20-44 *Spencer*
42-103004 A9-<u>A</u>		CL 3-3-44 *Johnson*
		MIA 5-28-44 *Clemovitz*
42-103008 C3-J		MIAc 3-21-44 *Watkins*
42-103289 B3-H	H.E. Scott	CL 5-2-44 *H. Scott*
42-103297 A9-		
42-103300 C3- "Nobody's Darling"		MIAc 5-24-44 *Service Grp*

P-51C-5-NT

42-103328 A9-M	A.J. Melancon	
42-103335 A9-S	B.W. Turner	MIA 6-20-44 *Turner*
42-103338 A9-		MIA 6-25-44 *Reetzke*
42-103340 A9-		
42-103591 B3-	J. Carter	CL 8-8-44 *Whited*
42-103613 C3-B "Green Hornet"	J.R. Stricker	

P-51B-5-NA

43-6330 A9- "Beachcomber"	G.T. McEachron	MIA 4-22-44 *Maxwell*
43-6332 C3-		MIA 4-15-44 *Cahill*
43-6360 C3-C "de-RUMBLE-izer"	R.E. Proctor	
43-6361 B3-	J. Carter	
43-6368 A9-X "It Sends Me"	M.M. Kellogg	
43-6377 C3-K "Quitcher' Kickin'"	B.B. Bingham	
43-6380 C3-F		
43-6382 C3-A		
43-6426 B3-W "Pegasus"	G.R. Doerr	MIA 4-22-44 *Doerr*
43-6434 B3-	D.L. Benbenek	MIA 3-20-44 *Benbenek*
43-6435 C3-O	J.W. Schmidt	MIA 3-4-44 *McGee*
43-6438 C3-M "Hoo Flung Dung"	R.C. McWherter	
43-6438 C3-U		MIA 6-25-44 *Winham*
43-6443 C3-		MIA 6-25-44 *Thompson*
43-6445 C3-		
43-6446 B3-C "Ginny/Ellie"	A.M. Mimler/A.H. Tait	MIA 7-4-44 *Scott*
43-6447 C3-T "Lady June"	J.A. Warner	

43-6449 A9-		B/O 2-29-44 *Molen*
43-6458 B3-A "Huntin' Trouble"	D.H. Culberson	
43-6458 B3- "Killer"	F.W. Trumbower	CL 5-24-44 *Dalglish*
43-6463 B3-D "Dee"	C.H. Smith	
43-6490 A9-D		
43-6492 C3-		MIA 3-4-44 *Theil*
43-6493 C3-		MIA 3-4-44 *Edwards*
43-6494 C3-		MIA 4-5-44 *Lewis*
43-6501 B3-		CL 2-29-44 *Howell*
43-6505 B3-F "Sugarfoot"	N.H. Jacobson	
43-6512 A9-X "It Sends Me"	M.M. Kellogg	MIA 7-4-44 *Reddig*
43-6513 A9-		MIA 4-29-44 *Hersberger*
43-6514 B3-	P.W. Wood	
43-6516 A9-A "Fool's Paradise III"	E.M. McCall	CL 2-26-44 *Snyder*
43-6522 B3- "Mr. X"	H.R. Howell/A.J. Reinhart	
43-6524 A9- "Windy City III"	W.M. Haynes	
43-6528 A9-		MIA 7-16-44 *Anderson*
43-6542 C3-J "Little Chris II"	M.A. Thompson	
43-6558 C3-		MIAc 3-30-44 *Parker*
43-6568 B3-I	W.R. Schmidt	
43-6568 B3-I "Tear Azz"	H.E. Pressnall	
43-6585 A9-		MIA 6-19-44 *Nicholas*
43-6619 B3-		MIA 3-4-44 *Owings*
43-6645 B3-		MIA 3-4-44 *Gustafson*
43-6647 B3-	J.M. Boland	MIA 5-24-44 *Schmidt*
43-6657 B3- "Little Jinnie"	V.T. Johnson	CL 5-24-44 *Johnson*
43-6658 B3-V "Lee II"	G.L. Recagno	CL 4-8-44 *Thoresz*
43-6659 B3-	W.A. Webb	
43-6689 A9-		MIA 4-8-44 *Fontes*
43-6691 B3-S "Squirrel"	C.L. Gallagher	MIAc 3-25-44 *Tyree*
43-6692 A9-		MIA 6-17-44 *Lyman*
43-6694 C3-		MIA 3-4-44 *Aldrich*
43-6702 A9-E	W.H. Steiner	
43-6703 A9-		MIA 7-4-44 *Oyler*
43-6706 A9-L	T.H. Killingsworth	
43-6711 B3-	E.H. Berglind	MIA 3-18-44 *Berglind*
43-6713 C3-V "Marion"	C.H. Shiff	
43-6715 B3-Y "Skyczar"	F.A. Munder	
43-6716 A9-J "Lolita"	J.R. Ulricson	MIA 5-11-44 *Bruce*
43-6738 C3-		MIAc 4-26-44 *Pawlak*
43-6744 B3-U	H.D. Knuppel/A.J. Reinhart	
43-6752 B3-	S.L. McRoberts	MIA 4-15-44 *McRoberts*
43-6761 C3-R "Queenie"	R.W. Asbury	MIA 4-9-44 *Pollard*
43-6769 B3- "Flipped Lid"	W.F. Miller	MIA 4-22-44 *Miller*
43-6797 B3-B "Snark"	C.E. Shea/D.E. Lowers	
43-6804 A9-Q	T.J. Tilson	MIA 4-29-44 *Owen*

43-6812 A9-		CL 2-29-44 *Moore*
43-6814 C3-		MIA 3-4-44 *Collins*
43-6817 A9-U	T.E. Hale	MIAc 3-29-44 *Hale*
43-6822 B3-	K.L. Jacobs	DCL 4-27-44 *Smutz*
43-6830 C3-X "El Malo Hombre"	W.E. Bullard	MIA 7-18-44 *Bullard*
43-6852 A9-		MIA 4-29-44 *Diya*
43-6859 C3-N "Rose O'Day"	J.H. Santarlasci	B/O 8-4-44 *Santarlasci*
43-6905 C3-H "Destiny's Tot"	D.L. Boatright	
43-6907 C3-U		
43-6919 B3-		MIA 3-4-44 *Sullivan*
43-6924 B3-		MIA 3-4-44 *Polley*
43-6930 A9-		B/O 5-4-44 *Carr*
43-6932 A9-V	N.F. Ullo	MIA 3-8-44 *Ullo*
43-6949 B3- "Lady Joan III"	C.H. Davis	MIA 6-17-44 *Johnson*
43-6950 A9-R	R. Benson	MIA 5-11-44 *Benson*
43-6951 B3-	L. Moyer	MIA 3-4-44 *Moyer*
43-6952 C3- "Donna Mae"	J. Robertson	MIA 6-21-44 *Hamilton*
43-6953 B3-	L.D. Smutz	MIA 7-11-44 *Myers*
43-6954 B3-H	H.E. Scott/P.H. Henry	
43-6964 C3-		MIA 8-13-44 *Rice*
43-6975 C3-		MIA 3-4-44 *Watson*
43-6979 B3-G "Tarheel Special"	D.R. Tucker	
43-6993 A9-		MIA 6-12-44 *Hollowell*
43-6994 B3-	H.W. Ringgenberg	ASR 4-15-44 *Ringgenberg*
43-6996 C3-<u>R</u>		
43-7001 A9-D		
43-7006 A9-N "Lil Bear"	W.A. McKinney	MIA 4-23-44 *Barlow*
43-7010 A9-	W.W. Huff	
43-7016 C3- "Frisco Kid"	R.D. Kunz	MIA 8-13-44 *Brooks*
43-7048 C3-		MIA 5-30-44 *Rook*
43-7056 B3-	W.A. Webb	B/O 7-25-44 *Jones*
43-7108 B3-U	H.D. Knuppel	MIA 7-4-44 *Gervan*

P-51B-10-NA

43-7138 B3-R "Rex"	E.J. Vesely	MIA 6-15-44 *Vesely*
43-7148 C3-		MIA 4-8-44 *Wenner*
43-7194 A9-I "Courser"	M.A. Kammerlohr	
43-7194 A9-E		
42-106435 A9-		MIA 6-11-44 *Vance*
42-106453 B3-S "Squirrel"	C.L. Gallagher	CL 4-8-44 *Wood*
		MIA 6-19-44 *White*
42-106466 B3-E "Sand and Sage"	W.W. Steinke	MIA 4-9-44 *Steinke*
42-106477 B3-		MIA 4-12-44 *Howell*
42-106481 C3-		MIA 5-28-44 *Wilson*
42-106485 A9-V "Maggie's Drawers"	A.G. Johnson	MIA 4-29-44 *Johnson*
42-106486 C3-A "Virginia"	R.B. McGee	MIA 5-28-44 *Ladas*

42-106488 A9-   MIA 4-11-44 *McKenna*
42-106616 B3-   H.W. Ringgenberg   MIA 5-24-44 *Smith*
42-106619 C3-R "Queenie II"   R.W. Asbury
42-106621 C3-X   R.M. Lamar
42-106629 B3-
42-106643 A9-   MIA 4-30-44 *Moore*
42-106645 A9- "Schubert's Serenade"   W.H. Schubert   CL 8-16-44 *Robinson*
42-106647 C3-D "Big Mac Junior"   J.R. Brown   MIA 8-8-44 *Brown*
42-106665 B3-   MIA 4-15-44 *Hare*
                (note-he was a 382nd pilot flying a 381st a/c on this date)
42-106671 C3-   MIAc 4-26-44 *Deeds*
42-106705 B3-V "Lee II"   G.L. Recagno   MIA 8-28-44 *di Zerega*
42-106720 B3-
42-106728 A9-
42-106729 B3-   V.T. Johnson   MIA 6-24-44 *Clark*
42-106731 B3-D "Dee"   C.H. Smith
42-106731 B3-F "Sugarfoot II"   N.H. Jacobson   MIA 7-4-44 *Doran*
42-106732 B3-
42-106734 B3-   J. Gervan/B.D. Williams
42-106737 C3-C   R.E. Proctor

P-51C-10-NT
43-25045 C3-W "My Pal Snookie"   E.T. Pawlak

P-51B-15-NA
42-106740 B3-Z "Honk Honk"   J.J. Thoresz
42-106743 B3-   J.E. Early
42-106765 A9- "Bless Bess"   R.R. Wisner
42-106772 B3-M "Lady Patricia"   G.B. Scott
42-106788 B3-
42-106795 A9-Z "Georgia Ann"   J.E. Hill   MIA 6-14-44 *Hill*
42-106822 B3-   J.M. Boland   MIA 6-17-44 *Kemmerer*
42-106834 B3-D   J.B. Dalglish   MIA 5-24-44 *Kennedy*
42-106837 B3-
42-106877 B3- "Suzabelle"   R.P. Lucas   MIA 5-24-44 *Lucas*
42-106887 C3-   F. Kozaczka   MIA 5-30-44 *Stearns*
42-106888 B3-   R.D. Freyermuth   MIA 6-29-44 *Wood*
42-106899 C3-C   R.E. Proctor   MIA 5-1-44 *Sykes*
42-106939 C3-   CL 6-17-44 *Williams*
43-24752 B3-E "Stinky"   C.F. Stuart   MIA 6-17-44 *Yochim*
43-24789 B3-   MIA 6-14-44 *Mimler*
43-24837 C3-W   E.T. Pawlak   B/O 6-10-44 *Palmer*

P-51D-5-NA
44-13309 A9-A "Fool's Paradise IV" E.M. McCall   MIA 8-9-44 *Morrison*
44-13310 A9- "Oklahoma Kid III"   B.R. Williams MIA 7-27-44 *Williams*

44-13327 B3-A "Huntin' Trouble II"	D.H. Culberson	MIAc 7-26-44 *Culberson*
44-13340 B3-S "Squirrel"	C.L. Gallagher	
44-13373 B3-U "Voodoo"	H.D. Knuppel	MIA 8-9-44 *McCowan*
44-13380 C3-M "Hoo Flung Dung"	R.C. McWherter	
44-13384 A9- "Little Chico"	D.W. Ray	
44-13396 B3-D	J.B. Dalglish	
44-13396 B3-D "One Long Hop"	C.E. Shea	
44-13405 B3-		
44-13408 C3-	D.L. King	
44-13548 B3- "Skywolf"	J. Carter	
44-13550 A9- "Windy City IV"	W.M. Haynes	
44-13554 C3-P "Roscoe II"	J.N. Brink	MIA 8-13-44 *Hudson*
44-13559 A9-M	A.J. Melancon	
44-13575 C3-	B.S. Irvin	
44-13587 A9- "Angels' Playmate IV"	E.P. Ballinger	MIA 8-26-44 *Nielsen*
44-13590 B3- "Frankie Boy"	J.M. Boland	
44-13605 A9-R	L.D. Morrison	
44-13606 A9- "Southern Belle II"	M.L. DeLong	
44-13622 B3- "Buster"	C.W. Lasko	
44-13634 C3-U		
44-13640 B3-		B/O 8-8-44 *Reinhart*
44-13644 B3-V "Lee III"	G.L. Recagno	
44-13644 B3-V "Sugarfoot III"	N.H. Jacobson	
44-13672 B3-I "Sword of the Spirit"	H.E. Pressnall	
44-13693 C3-H		
44-13697 A9-	H.B. Messer	
44-13706 A9-I "Courser II"	M.A. Kammerlohr	
44-13731 A9-T		CL 7-28-44 *Rolland*
44-13765 A9-A "Corky-Anne II"	G.C. Clough	
44-13774 B3-		CL 8-9-44 *Henry*
44-13777 A9-	H.E. Lavin	
44-13805 A9- "Diablo"	J.B. Tipton	
44-13816 C3-J		
44-13833 A9-		
44-13841 A9-O "Torque Jockey"		
44-13900 B3-		
44-13989 A9-B "Pat-Mary Pat"		
44-14005 C3-N		
44-14022 A9-N "Miss-Fire"	M.M. Kellogg	
44-14048 B3-A		
44-14059 B3-Y "Skyczar"	F.A. Munder	

380th Ftr Sqn Incomplete Codes/Serials

P-51B A9-F "Limited Service"	C.R. Reddig
P-51B A9-T "Honey Belle"	R.J. Tyler
P-51B A9-T "Ballzout"	R.J. Tyler

P-51B A9- "Windy City"	W.M. Haynes
P-51B A9- "Windy City II"	W.M. Haynes
P-51B A9-A "Corky-Anne"	G.C. Clough
P-51B A9- "Little Joe"	F. Clemovitz
P-51B A9- "Oklahoma Kid"	B.R. Williams
P-51B A9- "Oklahoma Kid II"	B.R. Williams
P-51B A9- "Southern Belle"	M.L. DeLong
P-51B A9- "Angel's Playmate"	E.P. Ballinger
P-51B A9- "Angel's Playmate II"	E.P. Ballinger
P-51B A9- "Angel's Playmate III"	E.P. Ballinger
P-51B A9- "Beachcomber II"	G.T. McEachron
P-51D A9- "Beachcomber III"	G.T. McEachron

381st Ftr Sqn Incomplete Codes/Serials

P-51B B3- "Damn Yankee"	E.W. Kemmerer
P-51B B3- "Hun Hunter"	
P-51B B3- "Old Missouri"	
P-51D B3-J "Mar Jean III"	

382nd Ftr Sqn Incomplete Codes/Serials

P-51B C3-P "Roscoe II"	J.N. Brink
P-51B C3-L "Princess Marge"	R.E. Schillereff
P-51B C3-V "El's Belle Ginny"	E.W. Odell
P-51B C3-G "The Mighty Midget"	J.H. Clark
P-51B C3- "Pied Piper"	D.H. Rook
P-51B C3- "Toni Girl"	L.D. Morrison
P-51B C3- "Pudge"	R.M. Heberlein
P-51B C3- "Gracious"	L.E. Webster
P-51D C3-A "Virginia"	R.B. McGee
P-51D C3- "El Don"	R.D. Kunz
P-51D C3- "Donna Mae"	J. Robertson
P-51B C3- "Dopey Gal"	
P-51D C3- "Betty Lou"	

Group Hack Aircraft

UC-78 43-7781
AT-23B 41-35758
L-4B 43-1405
Proctor Z-7199
Proctor HM288

Appendix 10
Non-Flying Personnel

The following pages contain rosters of the 363rd's non-flying personnel. While all Group and Squadron records were consulted, there may still be omissions or inaccuracies in ranks/positions.

Headquarters

Allen, Seward H., Capt. – Armament
Ashbaugh, Ralph D., Lt. – Medical
Axelrod, Bernard, Maj. – Flight Surgeon
Baro, Angelo, Lt. – Special Services
Bean, Frank M., Lt. – ??
Beall, Charles W., Capt. – Supply
Bethea, Alfred W., LtCol. – Exec
Bunker, Theodore C., Maj. – Supply
Clarke, Roger A., Lt. – Assistant IO
Cole, Gerard, Capt. – Chaplain
Cummens, Richard, Lt. – Communications
Dahl, Robert E., Lt. – Communications
Foster, Edward, Lt. – Medical
Foster, Robert K., Capt. – Chaplain
Hamilton, Warren, Capt. – IO
Hirzel, Fred R., Lt. – Assistant IO
Hollarbrush, Fred L., Lt. – Armament
Hudiburgh, Sydney, Lt. – ??
Jackson, Gilbert E., Capt. – Assistant Ops
Jorden, Thomas W., Capt. – ??
Lane, David, Capt. – Communications
McCloskey, Hugh J., Lt. – Ops
McLaughlin, Merrill M., Lt. – IO, Historical
McKennan, Bruce, Maj. – Adjutant
McWhirter, Hubert W., Maj. – IO
Moree, Herbert E., Capt.-Adjutant
Morris, Frank R., Maj. – Assistant Exec
Parsons, Harold M., Lt. – IO
Plagens, Lt. – ??
Raub, Ray B., Capt. – Statistical
Rehfus, Albert, Capt. – Communications
Rier, Robert G., Capt. – Engineering
Russell, Lew M., Capt. – Public Relations
Saunders, George C., Maj. – Flight Surgeon
Seigler, Charles E., Capt. – Adjutant
Shanley, John P., Capt. – Adjutant
Smith, Maj. – Flight Surgeon

Swink, Donald G., Lt. – Assistant Adjutant
Tavormina, Peter, Lt. – Weather
Taylor, Frank A., Lt. – Assistant Adjutant
Woods, John E., Capt. – IO
Yackman, Lt. – IO
Young, Robert L., Maj. – IO

Edmondson, Chad B., W/O – Assistant Adjutant
Horst, Urban J., W/O – Engineering

Dushan, Joseph – First Sergeant

M/Sgt
Jack W. Bennett   Paul Gerausi
Philip L. Griffiths   Charles W. Petty
Harold E. Pitts   Charles A. Springs

T/Sgt
Webster E. Blanchard   Ray T. Connors
Eddie C. Kennedy   Horace R. Lewis
Maynard A. Radke   Gene Salzman
James A. Spinney   Emerson A. Stairs
John S. Strong   Horace S. Wright

S/Sgt
Fletcher G. Bevis   Arthur Boisvert
Gilbert L. Hall   John W. Hart
James D. Haver   Cecil H. Jackson
Gordon J. Kuhlman   Donald P. LaBreck
Stephen Lefkovitch   Walter E. Leighninger
George F. Sardou   Charles C. Smith
Thomas Weigand

Sgt
George W. Dowling   William J. Doyle
Dominick L. Ferriero   George T. Henry
Lawton Irvine   Robert S. Jaczinski
Walter R. Klinksick   Thomas C. Lopes
Donald R. Putney   Robert J. Regendahl
Laverne G. Robertson   Francis D. Selig
Roy I. Stevens   Albert A. Weirwick

Cpl
Arthur V. Allen   Robert A. Batenhorst
Harvey C. Bremer-comm.   Norman H. Cowan
Earl T. Detlaff   R.V. Dickson

Delos W. Erickson-comm
Fred L. Gerry
J.W. Harris
James E. Lay
Willie G. Nuckolls
John Orphanus
Sewell R. Turner

Ray G. Fitzpatrick
John E. Haglund-comm
Francis J. Kratz
Jess F. Martin
Jack Oliveri
Earl W. Schnell
Luther R. Walton

PFC
George Banoff
Alven J. Flanders
Frank T. Kadji
Edward H. Littrell
Eugene E. Moss
Max J. Paulsen
Mark Rowan
Robert W. Taber

Charles M. Clark
Sterling B. Iverson
John Konstantowicz
Harold E. Mollus
John P. Murphy
Joseph Portanova
Henry C. Skarr-IO
Elver Voth

Pvt
John J. Allen
Eli Botwinick
John L. Cronin
John B. Kump
Jack M. Norris
Harvey K. Whaley

Thomas J. Allen
Trinidad Cevallos
Herman Holdbrooks
Ralph E. Neff
Herman W. Schaar

380th Fighter Squadron
Almquist, Fred E., Lt. – Armament
Brothers, Walter F., Lt. – Communications
Crowdis, Charles C., Lt. – Armament
DiMaio, Michael, Capt. – Flight Surgeon
Duecker, John C., Lt. – Supply
Erwin, James D., Lt. – Supply
Farrior, Edward M., Lt. – Camouflauge
Feigen, Albert J., Lt. – Assistant IO
Hammer, Edson G., Lt. – Adjutant, Radar
Kirk, John R., Lt. – Armament
Laney, George M., Capt. – Adjutant, Exec
Maciolek, John B., Lt. – Communications
Mayer, Robert J., Lt. – Assistant Engineering
McInturff, Herman, Lt. – Exec
Moneta, William, Lt. – Assistant IO
Muller, Wolfgang H., Lt. – Ordnance
Pruitt, Warren D., Capt. – IO
Rier, Robert G., Capt. – Engineering

Swenson, Carl E., Capt. – Engineering
Woods, John E., Capt. – IO

Hall, Gilbert L. – First Sergeant

M/Sgt

Dewey Austin-eng

Philip L. Griffiths

Charles E. Patton-eng

Clarence H. Cox-arm.

Myron E. Hineman-eng(Line Chief)

Arthur H. Voight-eng

T/Sgt

Richard L. Art-eng(prop)

Herman Gonski-eng

Thaddeus Kaminski

John F. Miller-eng(c/c)

Charlton N. Motley-eng(c/c)

John T. Talbot

William H. Gibson-arm.

Carlton E. Jeffcoat-comm

Claude D. May-eng(c/c)

Burl Mitchell-eng(c/c)

Walter H. Russell-arm.

John Vojta-eng

S/Sgt

Floyd K. Anderson-eng

Cecil E. Baker-eng(c/c)

Lewis E. Beyer-eng

Alfred J. Bjork-eng

Ben Blake-eng(c/c)

Charles D. Blossom-eng(ac/c & c/c)

James H. Bourne-arm.

Harold L. Burks-eng(c/c)

Joseph J. Cherniskey-arm.

Vincent A. Colter-eng

Arthur K. Conerton-eng(ac/c & c/c)

Erwin C. Derrick-eng(c/c)

Charles K. Fairfield-arm.

James C. Gaddy-arm.

Leonard V. Hackley-eng(c/c)

Edward J. Hart-comm

David A. Holbrook-eng(c/c)

Woodrow W. Jones-eng

Jack J. Kellar-eng(c/c)

Robert J. Lagerman-ord

John McCabe-eng(c/c)

William G. Mettin-comm

Howard E. Mosier-eng(c/c)

Bart C. O'Rourke-ord

Chester J. Podolak-eng

Howard E. Rowe-medical

Michael Salvage-eng(c/c)

James M. Auringer-eng(electrical)

Gabriel C. Berenson-comm

Franklin Biere-eng(c/c)

Eugene K. Black-eng(c/c)

Herman C. Blamiers-eng(electrical)

William G. Blount-eng(c/c)

John E. Braubach-eng(c/c)

Clarence B. Chase-eng

Clement Cleveland-comm

Clarence A. Colyer-eng(electrical)

Charles H. Cornell-eng(c/c)

Edward C. Egan-eng(c/c)

Jess W. Foster-eng(ac/c & c/c)

John C. Grady-eng

Anthony H. Haley-eng(c/c)

Wilfred S. Hicks-eng(ac/c & c/c)

Cecil H. Jackson-comm

Hilton C. Joyner

Cecil A. Kelly-eng(prop)

William J. McAndrews-IO

Albert J. McElroy-eng(c/c)

Carl Monday-eng(c/c)

Myron V. Mudd-Supply

Eugene E. Pelizzari-eng(c/c)

Harry F. Rice-eng(c/c)

Paul A. Ruttenberg-eng(c/c)

Robert P. Shay-arm.

Paul A. Snow-Ops
Rolland G. Thompson-transp
Edward F. Weidlich-eng(c/c)
Pearl R. Williams-eng(prop)
Jack B. Wilson-arm.
Alvin J. Wolff-eng(c/c)

Ollie P. Stone-eng(c/c)
Toi Toy-eng(sheet metal)
Lowell C. Williams-eng(c/c)
Ted Williams-eng(c/c)
Wallace W. Winkler-eng(c/c)
Thurman Works-transp

Sgt

William T. Ahern-eng(ac/c)
Robert J. Azevedo-eng.
William C. Barton-eng
Gabriel C. Berenson-comm
John F. Burns
Maximiliano Chavez-mess
Francis E. Collins-arm.
Gerald W. Day-arm.
Howard P. Elliott
Irwin J. Fine-comm
Ralph C. Fritz-eng
Leonard E. Geiger-HQ
Sam D. Griffin-eng
Tom F. Hanley-eng(ac/c)
Fidelis Herman-comm
Bernly K. Hinson-comm
Russell Jayne-arm.
Donald F. Judge-eng(sheet metal)
Milroy E. Lee-arm.
Franklin T. Lewis-ord
John L. Locklair-arm.
Sol W. Mallin-eng(ac/c)
Lloyd H. Miller-eng(ac/c)
Louis W. Mittler-eng
Oscar P. Mozingo
Henry G. Neinner-eng(ac/c)
Loren L. Outhouse-mess
Leon E. Prince-eng(ac/c)
Thomas J. Pymm-arm.
Wilbur B. Rigby-mess
John J. Salay-eng
Michael R. Seiber-arm.
Henry C. Skarr-IO
Fred Trommer-mess
Robert E. Watson-eng(ac/c)
Woodrow J. Whitson-ord
Glenn E. Wilson-eng(ac/c)

Robert C. Ahlstrom-comm
Jesse W. Barner-eng
Peter A. Bender-arm.
Edmund B. Borkowski-eng(ac/c)
Wayman A. Caldwell-eng(ac/c)
James M. Christensen-arm.
Billy J. Davis-eng(ac/c)
Leo A. Dregier-eng(ac/c)
Richard B. Engelman-ops
Willard J. Fitzgerald-ord
William A. Gallinis-ord
Joseph Giordano-eng
James R. Grossbohlin-comm
Henry – mess
Russell W. Hinds-arm.
John W. Hoffman
Vance J. Jenson-comm
Edward A. Kepka-comm
Stanley Lench-eng(ac/c)
Luther E. Lewis-arm.
Robert Majnik-eng(ac/c)
Clare H. McGlynn-arm.
Richard E. Miller-eng(ac/c)
Victor N. Moreno-eng
Clarence J. Myers-HQ
Robert T. Nelson-mess
Peter J. Pfau-comm
Mike W. Purcell-arm.
Maurice W. Richardson-comm
George W. Ryan-eng
Charles L. Sanner-comm
Jim C. Singleton-comm
Howard C. Stevens-eng(electrical)
William H. Van Arsdale-comm
Gilbert G. Whited-eng
Ivan O. Wick-arm.
Bernard A. Wolf-mess

Cpl

Rocco J. Albanese-transp

John H. Bailey-mess

Harold J. Benjamin-arm.

Stanley J. Boron-arm.

Robert H. Bowe-arm.

Edward C. Brokenshire-arm.

Leo Bruss-comm.

Robert L. Chugon-eng

William Cole-medical

Ignace Conte-arm.

Walter S. Doernburg-comm

Ivan R. Farris-transp

Robert L. Foley-ord

John M. Gaffney-comm

Harry O. Gentry-arm.

John G. Good-comm

Holdene J. Graves-arm.

Clayton W. Hasher-ord

George Hood-comm

Gilbert Jaramillo-eng

Roy B. Kerby-arm.

Joseph C. Kwoka-arm.

Ralph Lanteri-comm

Joseph Lazorski-comm

John P. Lee-HQ

Aaron Lipson-comm

Matthew B. McPartland-arm.

Thomas J. Murray-transp

Frank N. Osborne-arm.

Eugene Rayeur-mess

Alex S. Roethlisberger-arm.

Wallace P. Schulz-supply

John M. Sigmund-HQ

Roland D. Simpkins-eng

John A. Smith-eng

Vernon M. Tobaas

Chester J. Tryburczy-arm.

Donald J. Van Sluyters-arm.

Jesse M. Webb-arm.

Alvin J. Willis-mess

Joseph A. Amico-HQ

Lester I. Barclay

William R. Betsill-ord

James Boudros-HQ

Michael Brady-comm

Kenneth H. Brooks-comm

Arthur C. Carlson-arm.

James H. Church-chem

Francis E. Collins-arm.

James F. Delaney-arm.

William H. Evans-arm.

John M. Ferriera-arm.

Alvin J. Franders

William M. Gatton-comm

Fred I. Gerry-HQ

Michael J. Gorham-eng(ac/c)

John C. Hackett-arm.

Seth E. Hickerson-eng(electrical)

Francis J. Hope-comm

Glenwood N. Kelso-comm

Robert L. Kirkman-mess

Anthony C. Lamarca-arm.

Harry R. Larch-comm

James B. Leach

William E. Lindberg-medical

John J. McNurlen-eng

Victor M. Morales-comm

Arnold J. Newcomer-ord

Stan J. Pietrasiewicz-eng

Herbert H. Roeger-arm.

Rene A. Roy-medical

Joseph D. Sciacca-ops

Henry H. Simokat-eng(sheet metal)

Walter Smaga-arm.

Harry L. Strausser-arm.

George W. Trombley-medical

Paul Van Dyken-comm

Lewis M. Wadley-ord

William F. Wheeler-eng

PFC

Arthur V. Allen-medical

Fiore C. Ansonia

Philip H. Berry-ord

Stanley Adams-ord

Thomas J. Baumgarden-medical

Willard B. Blackwell-eng

Paul C. Bramlet – arm.
James W. Brown-eng
William O. Chambers-medical
Robert L. Cook-IO
Ray Del Greco
Buron N. Eubanks-mess
Rodolfo Flores-mess
Wallace R. Griss-supply
John W. Hopper
Cecil O. Kelly-eng
Paul W. Paig
Frank A. Serio-comm
Henry Soto-transp/mess
Walter G. Stanford-eng
Donald Von Fossen-ord
John A. Winters-arm.
Fernando R. Zaragoza-mess

Joseph P. Bricarello-arm.
James F. Callejas
Salvatore A. Congilose-ord
Philip C. Couch
Ernest S. Enos-medical
George E. Fiebe
Valerte S. Gonzales
William H. Hedges
Edward G. Humeny-ord
John J. Noon-ord
Vernone E. Paige-arm.
Weldon R. Snively-ops
Norman L. Speed
David Von Fossen-ord
Edgar A. Wagner-eng
James A. Woody-eng

Pvt

Andres Bonnot-mess
George W. Crist-ord
Grover C. Harper
Ravalli S. LaBatte-ord
Mitchell-eng
Thomas L. Robinson
Raleigh C. Shifflot-eng

Jesse O. Buchanan-comm
Norman M. Daniels-medical
Edward G. Kelly-comm
Clarence Minthorn
Leland H. Moore-mess
Howard E. Ryan-eng
Harold Snyder-mess

381st Fighter Squadron

Ashbaugh, Ralph D., Capt. – Flight Surgeon
Clarke, Roger A., Lt. – IO
Decker, George J., Capt. – Engineering
Elfenbein, Abraham, Lt. – Equipment
Gentry, Byron B., Capt. – IO
Hendricks, Lt. – IO
Kirby, Robert D., Lt. – Adjutant
Lane, David, Capt. – Communications
LeBlanc, Julian M., Capt. – Adjutant
Legaskis, James, Capt. – Exec
McManus, James J., Lt. – Armament
Safos, Arthur F., Lt. – Communications
Saunders, George C., Capt. – Flight Surgeon
Siegel, Edwin G., Capt. – Statistical
Smith, Casper W., Lt. – ??
Taylor, Frank A., Lt. – Adjutant
Vier, Jack L., Lt. – Supply

Wolf, David A., Lt. – Assistant IO

Ziger, Jerome A., Lt. – Armament

Connors, Ray T. – First Sergeant

M/Sgt

Michael Anuzis-arm. chief

Clifford F. Hauch-Eng. Chief

Lewie A. Fear-eng

Neils E. Petersen-eng(Line Chief)

T/Sgt

Fred W. Binns

John E. Buman-eng(c/c)

Gerard L. Halle-eng(c/c)

Cleo A. Longton-eng(c/c)

Walter A. Matoske-eng

Alex Slutsky-arm.

Gerald W. Upton-arm.

Stephen G. Borden-eng(c/c)

Frank J. Dolce

Richard C. Johnson-arm.

James L. Koch-eng

James L. Ross-eng

Jackie W. Smythe-arm.

S/Sgt

Carroll C. Andrinks-arm.

Archie D. Baland

Warren H. Bennett-eng(c/c)

Bernard J. Blechinger-eng(c/c)

Paul F. Braham-arm.

Stephen P. Churilla-eng(c/c)

Anton J. Cocek-eng(c/c)

William Decho-eng(ac/c & c/c)

Robert M. Ellingson-transp

James F. Evans-eng(c/c)

David Ferguson-eng

Frank B. Gilligan-eng(c/c)

Fred M. Greene-eng

Harold Hansen-eng(c/c)

Edward O. Hennig

Roy W. Hoover-eng(c/c)

D.L. Jackson-eng(c/c)

Robert F. Keller-eng

Allen S. Kotler

Bernard Leon-eng(c/c)

Anthony P. Mandernack

Leo F. Manning-arm.

Gerald J. Martin-eng

Warren L. McCoy-electrical

Paul D. Monte-eng

Thomas J. O'Connell

John T. Phillips

Oliver D. Autrey

Wendell H. Benkosky

Guy E. Bishop-prop

Arthur A. Boisvert-supply

Nicholas Chuma-Tech supply

Kenneth R. Clark-eng(c/c)

Charles V. Cornwell

Stephen J. DeMarco-eng(c/c)

Ralph D. Ervin-eng(c/c)

Michael Fekete-eng(c/c)

William K. Fogle

Wallace T. Goodhue-eng(c/c)

Elmer L. Hansen-eng(c/c)

Van W. Hawkins-arm.

Ralph B. Hill-radar

Donald J. Horine-eng

Hayden W. Jones-prop

Philip Kilpatrick

Weldon A. Lee-eng(c/c)

Jacque E. Lewis-eng(c/c)

Lester G. Mann-eng

Dominic F. Marazzo-eng(c/c)

Leroy A. Matousek-eng

William B. Meyer-eng

Clyde Nitch-ord

Lewis W. Owen

Thomas I. Reese-eng

Eugene A. Renneker-eng
Johnny H. Sanford
James W. Shaw-eng
Jack Smith-arm.
Elmer W. Staten-eng(ac/c & c/c)
Oscar H. Strum
William P. Turner-eng(c/c)
Albert A. Weirick
John White-eng(c/c)

Byron Sandlin-eng(c/c)
James J. Schwartze
Milton L. Sims-eng
Roger F. Sommer
John Stroia-eng
Robert S. Tomlinson-eng
Harold K. Wachestork-eng
Ralph A. Whitacre-sheet metal
Roscoe J. Wooten-sheet metal

Sgt

Donald A. Baird-arm.
Herbert H. Braun-parachute
Joseph W. Brown
Theodore Cohen-eng
Riley H. Courreges-eng(ac/c)
Henry E. Curtis-supply clerk
Elvin H. Eyler-eng
Jacob Fradkin-eng
Charles V. Furness-eng
Maynard E. Glidden-classification
Frank J. Grapelis
Harold H. Hass-arm.
Lawrence Hestand-eng
Roy W. Hoover
Billy J. Johnson
Delton F. Kuntz-eng
Wilbur R. Lundy-arm.
Donald B. Mathena-eng
Irvin Meinken-eng
Forrest Monner-eng
Walter P. Morris
Matthew E. Paradowski
Leroy A. Petousek-eng
Kenneth L. Prior-eng
Elton L. Ritchey-eng(ac/c)
John C. Roussell-arm.
Arnold B. Shafer-eng
Dominick J. Siniscalchi-eng
Herbert P. Southern-mess
Bernard J. Stern
Kenneth K. Thach-eng(c/c)
Wilton T. Turner-eng(ac/c)
Joseph A. Villa-mess
Rayford O. Warren-mess

Orlean I. Boen-arm.
William C. Brown-fuel crew
Joseph E. Cerulli-auto mechanic
George E. Conley
Francis R. Cummings
Glenn F. Egan
James E. Fitzgerald-arm.
Leo M. Frankenfield
Maillard A. Ginther
Earl W. Greene-eng
Norman J. Hance-teletype
Richard B. Heath-arm.
James J. Hoffman
Lester R. House-eng
John F. Kelly-arm.
John P. Lane
Nicholas Marinelli-eng(ac/c)
Charles T. McCormick-radio
Herbert W. Miller
James W. Moreland
Charles W. Moyle-arm.
George J. Payin
Robert D. Poole-eng
Bernard J. Quinn-arm.
William L. Rogers
Robert M. Scott
Joseph F. Shull-arm.
Clinton K. Smith-arm.
Warren C. Spitzer-eng
Arthur Sullivan
Martin V. Tilley-eng(ac/c)
Gerald W. Upton-arm.
Earl L. Vincent
Ted F. Wetzel-mess

Cpl

Frank M. Alvarez-medical

Chester K. Bobbitt

Alfred Buck

Ted Cohen-eng

Franklin D. Constantino-mess

Joseph R. Costello

Louis E. Cox

Joseph G. Dicker-arm.

Paul F. Engle-sheet metal

George C. France-arm.

Ferdinand Ganiarillas

Jess Green-arm.

Horace B. Hall-adminstration

Robert W. Heyne-arm.

Karl F. Hoffbauer-arm.

Sterling B. Iverson-administratiom

Robert P. Keller-eng

Norman E. Lee-arm.

Nicholas Litterio-arm.

Jesse Martin-medical

Thomas G. McKay-arm.

Larry E. Meeks

Russell J. Moren-mess

Lawrence E. Morris-eng

Durwood F. O'Shea-arm.

Edward P. Piglowski

Charles Roe

Milton L. Sims-eng

Thomas M. Sorrells

Samuel D. Swift-carpenter

Valerio J. Valeri

William W. West

Haynes Williams-arm.

William Yargee

Peter H. Bedrosian-arm.

William L. Bradaric-arm.

Miguel R. Calderon-arm.

Fred B. Colburn

Howard A. Cook

Ray E. Cottrill-radio

William Decko-eng

Wren J. Dillard-arm.

Lester H. Fields

Samuel A. Furman-eng

John H. Goss

Frank R. Hackel-arm.

Van W. Hawkins-arm.

Herbert W. Hill

Donald J. Horine-eng

Irving E. Jones-arm.

Arthur Kelsey-arm

Robert A. Lewis-arm.

Edward N. Maddox

Robert F. Martinez

Horace A. McKeever

Fillipo J. Mirasole-eng

Paul D. Monte-eng

James C. Nisbet-arm.

Jerry L. Perrotta

Stephen C. Quiroz

Lester Salzwedel-arm.

Billy E. Smith

Harry J. Steinberg

Hugh W. Teague-fuel crew

Edward H. Walczak-arm.

Denzil L. Whalen-Tech supply

John L. Williams-ord

PFC

Stanton J. Abel-arm.

William S. Bates

Henry H. Bergman-arm.

Kay O. Dennis

Joseph G. Dwyer

Lawrence K. Fong

Steve Gentilcore

Horace P. Hall

Wilton A. Mahoffey-eng

Edward Ayres

Arthur A. Bazzonotti-arm.

Frank D. Collins

Frank M. Duckworth-arm.

John P. Fannon

Albert A. Gabriel

Herbert W. Haase-arm.

Wallace A. Knox

Edward J. McGaffney-arm.

Carlos Mendoza-eng
John L. Paul
Chester D. Read

Juan B. Pacheco
John S. Phillips
Clyde J. Zuber

Pvt
Johnny C. Dobbs
Elias E. Downs
Epimonio Maes
George C. McDonald
Ralph Neff-medical
Hulon A. Sanders
Joseph E. Waddell

Jimmie Carroll
Paul L. Leemon
Edward Majusky
Alfred J. Miller-arm.
George J. Pollack
Louis Ventimiglia

382nd Fighter Squadron
Arey, Joseph C., Capt. – Exec
Ashbaugh, Ralph D., Lt. – Flight Surgeon
Axelrod, Bernard, Capt. – Flight Surgeon
Buckle, Richard, Capt. – Adjutant
Edwards, Edward, Lt. – Assistant Engineering
Foster, Edward, Capt. – Flight Surgeon
Harms, Harry J., Lt. – Communications
Harris, William P., Lt. – Engineering
Hollarbrush, Fred L., Lt. – Armament
Johnson, Norman P., Lt. – IO
Kiernan, Lawrence S., Lt. – Armament
LeBlanc, Julian M., Capt. – Adjutant
Maciolek, John B., Lt. – Transportation
McCluskey, Hugh J., Lt. – Ops
McManus, James D., Lt. – Ordnance
Mucci, Louis, Lt. – Communications
Parsons, Harold M., Lt. – IO
Reichart, Irving F., Lt. – Supply
Ross, Gilbert G., Lt. – ??
Turfle, Henry A., Lt. – Adjutant
Valentine, Herbert S., Capt. – IO

Smith, Ernest W. – First Sergeant

M/Sgt
Herbert O. Pacholke-arm.
Wayne H. Venable-eng

Charles E. Patton-eng

T/Sgt
Brown Barnett-eng(c/c)
Ralph L. Christensen-eng(Line Chief)
Richard N. Loyd

Vincent A. Colter-eng
Glyn H. Evans
Wilson W. McDaniel-Mess Sgt.

Cyrus H. Milby-eng(Flight Chief)

James P. Quinn-eng(Flight Chief)

Avelino Valdez-arm.

George E. Puro-arm.

Arthur P. Symons-eng(c/c)

S/Sgt

Walter F. Barker-eng(c/c)

Harold F. Becraft-supply

Arthur F. Belinski-eng

Walter F. Borowski-ops clerk

Joseph P. Campbell

Paul R. Carey

Charles C. Dartt-eng.(c/c)

Joseph F. Dix-arm.

Earle R. Dorr

Morris E. Easterly-eng(c/c)

Ernest L. Elmer-eng(c/c)

Gordon E. Garner-eng(c/c)

George A. Hess-eng(c/c)

George F. Jarecki-eng(c/c)

Donald P. LaBreck

Raymond T. Lien

Alex P. Lux-eng(c/c)

Joseph E. McDonald-eng(c/c)

Richard A. O'Connor-eng(c/c)

Martin E. Organtini-eng(c/c)

Swan L. Pederson-eng

Walter A. Prosneick-eng(c/c)

James W. Reagor

John L. Ross-eng(c/c)

Kenard J. Slocum-eng(c/c)

Alfred W. Swift-eng(c/c)

Homer P. Tunger-eng(c/c)

Ray L. Williams-eng(c/c)

Robert W. Yates-eng(c/c)

Joseph M. Beaner-eng(c/c)

Joseph N. Bellucci-arm

Robert Bly-supply

William S. Buffalo-radio

George A. Campbell-eng

Robert J. Coffman-arm.

John M. Day

Frank Dobbs

William F. Drew-eng

Emanuel Ehlenberger-eng(c/c)

Morton A. Fox-radar

Hollis T. Gillespie-arm.

David L. Holzner

Charles H. Krupp-eng(elect)

Charles M. Land

George P. Linkinhoker-eng(c/c)

Harold A. Magers-eng

Harry O. Nothnagel-eng(c/c)

Gerald L. Orem-instrument

John W. Pacey-eng(ac/c & c/c)

Robert A. Peterson-eng(c/c)

Richard A. Quinn-eng(c/c)

James P. Romeo-eng(prop)

Robert G. Ross-eng(c/c)

Charles E. Slonaker

Kenneth Thach-eng(c/c)

Richard Wagner-eng

Kenneth B. Wright

Sgt

Rolland A. Bassett-eng

Theodore A. Beach-eng

Paul J. Bernke-eng

Donald W. Brothers

Joseph F. Cateriniccha-arm.

Cyrus O. Christensen-eng(ac/c)

Leroy E. Conkle-supply

Robert S. Cope

Robert C. Craft-arm.

Stanley O. Day

Wayne T. Bates

Larry E. Benson

Robert J. Binger

Jesse R. Burks-eng(c/c)

Morton B. Chandler-eng(elect)

Lynn C. Christensen

Karl V. Cole-fuel crew

Robert Cota-arm.

Raymond E. Craig

Donald L. Dunning

Peter T. Eglinton-eng(ac/c)
James H. Ford-eng(ac/c)
John J. Gardner-fuel crew
James G. Gillen-arm.
Howard E. Guinther-med
George J. Henning-fuel crew
William L. Hughes-arm.
John E. Kallen
Charles E. Kennedy
John Kokladas-IO
Frank X. Lewis
Lauren K. Lymburner
James M. McQuate-eng(ac/c)
James A. Murphy-photo
Lonzo F. Nix-mess
Andrew O'Hanlon-eng(c/c)
Joseph J. Petrusick-eng(ac/c & c/c)
John E. Quilitzsch-eng.(ac/c)
Harold J. Roberts-arm.
Howard S. Rudoff-eng(ac/c)
Baxter C. Shepard
Carl W. Spurr-arm.
Delbert F. Teeter-ops
William J. Trainer-parachute
Elver Voth-IO clerk
Albert E. Zumpano-eng

Paul Fedak
Meyer M. Friedman-radio
Stanley L. Gardner-eng(ac/c)
James A. Goglucci
Robert C. Heine-arm.
Lyle F. Hicks
Harold W. Jones-arm.
Michael A. Kaza-comm.
Rudolph Klare-arm.
Robert W. Kunze-eng(prop)
Aloysius F. Litz
Lester A. McPheeters-Duty NCO
Paul F. Minehan-eng(ac/c)
Fred W. Nelson-eng(ac/c)
Frank J. Novak-camera
Roy C. Olhoeft-Tech supply
John F. Poythress-eng(ac/c)
Samuel R. Ramirez
Philip J. Rodger
Michael W. Scirocco-eng(ac/c)
Robert J. Spivey
Theodore K. Stark
Thompson – transp
Carmello J. Ventura
Carroll E. Yerg-arm.

Cpl

Clyde J. Anderson
Garfield J. Ausmus-arm.
Joseph F. Bates-eng clerk
Harvey H. Bowles-fuel crew
Dario A. Capacasa
Forrest D. Cowan-arm.
Walter S. Doernberg
Allan L. Driver-arm.
John J. Good
Murray L. Greif
James B. Hartley
Jack R. Hostetter-ambulance driver
Norris I. Hulvey-arm.
John P. Ivancie
O.L. Jones
H. Kines-arm.
Adrine D. Laraway-arm.
Edward P. Lepore-eng(ac/c)

William H. Anderson-clerk
William B. Baker
Harry W. Boone
James L. Cain-cook
Lawrence A. Casper
Kenneth G. Crowley-arm.
Daniel F. Donovan-admin clerk
William A. Galetich-ops
Joseph W. Gray-eng(ac/c)
Kenneth C. Hart-arm.
Morgan D. Hastings-eng(ac/c)
James E. Huffman-arm.
Marvin E. Humphrey
Wade Johnson
John J. Keenan
Frank J. Kowalik-arm.
Jack W. Larson-arm.
Thomas C. Lopes-medical

George D. Lucas
John J. Mahoney-arm.
Clifford A. McKinley-arm.
Peter Nichols-tech supply
Lloyd A. Phinney-arm.
Terance R. Read
Clarence R. Rothbrock
Thomas W. Rush-arm.
Andrew L. Scorsolini
Peter Sikula-eng(ac/c)
Robert T. Somers
Charles R. Stark
Frank C. Swickheimer-arm.
Fred L. Thomas
Salvatore J. Vaccaro-arm.
John C. Williamson-arm.
Bruce S. Young-arm.
George M. Zimberg-stat clerk

Robert H. MacGown-fuel crew
John E. Matheson-arm.
Samuel Nafshun-carpenter
Edward D. O'Connell
Edward Pollack-arm.
Joseph J. Ronczka
Ray H. Rumiser-arm.
Jerome Schwartz-arm.
Joseph D. Signore-clerk
Earl D. Snell
Clovis J. Starnes-arm.
Thomas H. Strzynski-arm.
George W. Synoground-arm.
Joseph M. Upperman-arm.
Melbourne F. Williams
Alfred P. Woodward-eng
Adrian C. Zielke-arm.

PFC

Austin Abell
Claude Burnett
Robert A. Coates-arm.
Marvin E. Ervin-eng(ac/c)
Alfred Gaskamp
Lee L. Harner-arm.
Farris B. Mansfield-fuel crew
Robert F. Mooney-decontamination operator
Wilbert E. Rolf-arm.
Mack Smith-fuel crew
Hugh D. Walton

Edward E. Blanchard
Ray C. Chlebowski
Paul H. Cornett
Paul A. Furbay
Thomas N. Genovese
Fred W. Keil
Vincent J. Marrese-eng

Norman C. Smart
Charles W. Snyder-transp

Pvt

Albert H. Berry
Jack Cutler
Haywood O. Denton
James C. Gaddy-arm.
Kenneth W. Heschke
Walter H. Krause
Meyer I. Miller
Norman C. Spurgeon
Robert F. Trevor
Earl D. Walker
Roland W. Winchell

Vincent J. Bertulli
William L. Davis-arm.
Jack Dockins
Lee W. Gullan-eng(ac/c)
Hugh L. Knight-cook
Peter Kuchman
John P. Murphy-radio
Argle C. Toon
James A. Trinka
Jack P. Wheeler

Appendix 11
Short Articles

The following pages contain a series of short articles describing events which took place in the 363rd's history. These are written by former members of the group, and it is hoped they will provide a more personal glimpse into the life and times of the unit.

The Blackest Day – March 4, 1944

The 363rd had 11 pilots MIA on this date and their loss has been a controversy since that time. Several members of the 363rd shared their recollections of that fateful day.

John Ulricson, Group CO: "I did not fly that one according to my combat log. As I recall, bad weather and our relatively inexperienced (in bad weather as well as other things) pilots accounted for our losses. I do not recall any particular problems with the German Air Force."

Concurring with Col. Ulricson's statement on the lack of instrument flight training, James Brink (382nd) had this to say: "The original pilots inability to fly safely under the weather conditions we encountered in England were the direct result of lack of actual weather flying training. Fourth Air Force, which was our command in California, prohibited us from flying the P-39 under actual weather conditions. Although I strongly criticize that policy, it was nevertheless a practical policy when you consider the 'state of the art' IFR WEATHER flying at that period of aeronautical history."

David Wolf, 381st Intelligence Officer: "At the time I was rooming with Lt. William Schmidt, a New Yorker, who became one of our very best fighter pilots in the 381st prior to his death. Bill was No. 4 man in the flight consisting of Lts. Louis Moyer, Burr H. Sullivan, and Theodore Owings. Bill was the only one that returned. He told me they were in this terrible solid overcast from 500 feet to 26,000 feet and they were flying on the leader, which I believe was Moyer. He had a feeling that something was not right and pulled off the tail end of the formation, almost immediately coming out of the overcast just over the water. He said he saw some flames on the water although he could not identify any aircraft or aircraft parts. It was his feeling that the other three had gone into the Channel after becoming disoriented in the overcast."

Richard Asbury, 382nd pilot: "I was flying Aldrich's wing on March 4. Two others from our flight had aborted early in the flight, soon after take-off. Aldrich and I were flying formation on the lead flight led by Willie Collins. Soon after take-off, we entered a solid wall of clouds from the surface up to high altitude. After a short while in the clouds we had reached approximately 7-8 thousand feet. I sensed something wrong with the increasing rush of air over the aircraft and I looked up at my flight instruments and we were in a right spiral with the altimeter unwinding rapidly. The airspeed indicator showed about 375 and increasing. I knew I had to leave the formation and I did. I struggled to right my aircraft and finally did at a very low altitude of about 300-400 feet above the water. It was a very ragged ceiling with some clouds looking like they went right down to the water. I saw no other aircraft but I did see a fire on the water and I heard one "May Day" call faintly. I answered with no response. As soon as I broke out under the clouds I took up a reciprocal course and weaving through the clouds made my way back to Rivenhall. None of the others returned and although I saw no aircraft go in the sea, I am 99.9% sure that is what happened to Aldrich, Edwards, Watson, Theil, McGee, and Collins."

Going Overseas

Herbert Valentine was the 382nd Intelligence Officer when the group went overseas. He describes his unique experience in getting to England.

"It seemed like a good idea to many of us at our embarking staging area, Camp Kilmer, New Jersey, to get a skinhead haircut. My reward for this great idea was pneumonia. I was so sick when we boarded the Queen Elizabeth that someone had to carry my pack up the gangplank, but I didn't want to be left behind and get assigned to a strange unit.

Our crossing was uneventful, but we couldn't help thinking of U-boats for we were unescorted and there were 17,000 men aboard. The Queen Elizabeth was fast, however, and it changed course every minute or so, making it virtually impossible for U-boats to zero in on her. I heard all this zigging and zagging only made our voyage about 5% longer.

As usual, the officers fared well, with 8-10 of us in a cabin designed for a couple. The enlisted men were a number of decks below where it was dark and motion was more noticeable. Officers took turns descending into the dark hole and trying to keep up the morale of the enlisted personnel. They also gathered in the main lounge where there was always poker games raging, some for big stakes. Fighter pilots were among the heaviest rollers; they had more money than others, and they played like there was no tomorrow.

My recollections of the voyage are hazy. I was feverish, disoriented, had constant, severe chills so that I spent a good deal of time in a hot bath. I recall an emergency drill when everyone went on deck. Everyone except me, who remained in my hot tub despite threats of court martial from the guards who came to roust me out.

We were served two meals a day. I remember going to my 5 o'clock seating one day only to find the dining room locked and dark. Didn't matter; I wasn't hungry anyway, so I returned to my sack. Later I learned that I had gone to the mess hall at 5 in the morning, thinking it was 5 in the evening.

None of the other officers realized how sick I was. The Group Medical Officer, one of my cabin mates, kept telling me I was seasick, but I knew I wasn't. Finally, I reported to the Naval medical facility, but was too tired to wait for a consultation, and went back to my cabin. A Navy medic noted my departure and listed me as a pneumonia suspect. A Navy medical officer followed up on me and found me the night before we landed in Glasgow in my cabin, out of my mind, weighing 153, and with a high fever.

Sulfa was new in those days, and the medics didn't know much about their new 'miracle drug'. But they figured they had little to lose with me, so gave me an initial dose of 12 tablets ... and in the morning my fever had broken. After a 6-day crossing, we landed in Glasgow on December 20, and I was the first off, lowered over the side in a basket to an ambulance on the dock. I was in the Glasgow hospital for three weeks.

Still weak and tired, I was discharged from the hospital one night and deposited at the train station to make my way back to my unit. All I can remember is the dampness and gloom of English railroad stations in the fog and blackouts and the grubbiness of larger industrial centers.

Mostly what I remember of that winter of 43/44 was cold Quonset huts, dreary English weather, powdered foods and Brussel sprouts, which the British seemed to have an unending supply of. Then there was my second bout with pneumonia. They debated on sending me back to the States as 'unfit for this climate', but when I got better they decided to give me another go, and I had no further health problems."

Intelligence Department

Herb Valentine continues with an overview of his job as Intelligence Officer.

"I found my work as Intelligence Officer of the squadron fascinating. Mostly it consisted of reading voluminous intelligence reports from all sorts of sources, and then calling to the attention of my commanding officer or the pilots that information which might be helpful to them. Training was also a major part of my job.

For example, pilots needed training in instant recognition of friendly and enemy aircraft. From every imaginable source, I obtained photos of aircraft and had them converted into slides. Then I projected them for the pilots at various speeds, some as high as a tenth of a second. They learned to recognize instantly the silhouettes of aircraft from every angle. The only problem with this training game was that some pilots would memorize my slides, so that I had to constantly seek new photos.

Another training exercise involved identification of landmarks. Pilots needed to know as many of them as possible. In thick cloud cover, and with the disorientation of combat, it was easy for pilots to lose their bearings. This was an especially critical problem for those who had been over Europe and were trying to find their way back to base in England. If they 'missed' England on the way back and flew out over the Atlantic.

So it was my job to teach geography-cities, rivers, and coastlines in Europe – as well as shapes of harbors and airdromes they might encounter as they returned from a mission over Germany. 'If you cross a harbor on the coast that looks like a broken elbow', I would say, 'that's Ostend, in Belgium. From there, take a vector of 260 degrees and you'll soon be back home.'

Another responsibility was to give pilots what information was available on escape routes and techniques, should they be shot down over occupied territory. This information was based on accounts of Allied pilots who made it back. Surprisingly, a few did, including some who were shot down over Germany and made it all the way through with help from the Underground."

Shot down!

Following are a few descriptions from pilots concerning their loss in combat. Also, at the end, a couple examples of Missing Aircrew Reports are given.

Neill Ullo, 380th, March 8, 1944: "On March 8, my birthday, it was the first mission fighters escorted the bombers all the way to Berlin. We did rendezvous that day and while escorting, my flight of Lts. Thomas Tilson, Roy Benson, Lloyd Bruce, and myself were attacked by a Me-109 and I received a shell burst off my left canopy window. I was blinded and the airplane went out of control, due to damage, I presume. I tried a blind spin recovery, felt it go like another spin in the opposite direction, decided to bail out and finally did. I found the canopy release and sensed it blowing away. I was going to release the seat belt and then remove the oxygen mask and throat mike, then jump out of the cockpit toward the extremity of the right wing as shown in training manual cartoons. But, when I released my safety belt I was gone! I felt a slight jerk as I left the plane. Then I was concerned about deploying the chute. I was tumbling blind through space. I reached for the rip cord which all through training was near my left shoulder. But, it wasn't there. Then I remembered a training session in which they said a pilot had clawed through his leather jacket on the wrong side trying to find the rip cord handle. So I tried the other side but it wasn't there either. Finally I remembered we were using British back pack chutes and the rip cord was in the center stomach area. I tried there and found it, jerked it, and handle cable and all was in my hand and the chute opened and after swinging violently from side to side it settled down and I regained my vision finally. I had started at 28,000 feet and I estimate the chute opened about 5,000 feet. I was drifting backwards toward a forest of tall skinny pines. But I was so glad to be in the open chute that I didn't worry about the landing until I entered the trees, passed the tops and the chute collapsed in the quiet air. Soon I was plummeting rapidly through the trees. I thought I was going to land very hard so I grabbed the shrouds above my head and tried to pull downward when I was about to hit the ground. When I did so I felt the chute miraculously fill and I landed in the snow as soft as could be. But, when I tried to stand up I found that I could not. The jerk I felt when leaving the plane was actually, as I found out later, my back being broken from a compressed fracture as I hit the violent air stream.

To make a long story short, I was captured by German troops who saw my descent. They transported me with my broken back to the nearest village jail, then to interrogation and thence to the Herman Göring hospital in Berlin. I was there on my back in bed for three months. Was sent to Frankfurt for solitary and interrogation, and eventually to Stalag Luft 3 POW camp."

Charles Stuart, 381st, describes the loss of William Schmidt, considered by many to be the best pilot in the squadron, on May 24, 1944

"If you look at the back of your right hand, your first finger would be a fellow named Shea, the next would be Schmidt and the third finger would be this new replacement (Robert Kennedy-author). I was on the far right. We had passed over some trees and then all of a sudden there was a German airfield right in front of us. The thing was sort of pear-shaped. Shea was way over on the left side. He was nearly a quarter of a mile from me – we were spread well out. Schmidt was in there and he kept calling this boy to 'get off my wing'. The guy was flying right on his wing, close formation, just a couple feet off the ground. I mean, that's suicide to fly like that; you need to spread out so you have a little maneuvering room. I hit the field up at the narrow end-the little end of the pear-and when I saw the thing there was a flak tower sitting right square in my gunsight. They didn't even see me coming. I recall it had three or four 20mm on it – maybe ten men manning the thing – and they were raring back and shooting like the devil at Schmidt and that wingman out in the middle of the field. Shea was little bit out of their range. They got the boy before I got them. I don't know whether they actually hit the new man or whether he got scared and flipped left and flew into Schmidt. Anyway, the two of them went across that field in one great hellish ball of flame and a split second later I hit my trigger and cleaned that platform out like a bowling ball knocks a strike down the alley. I think I knocked every one of them off that platform, but just a hair too late. That was about enough for Shea and me that day. We both revved back on the stick and got up high to 15 or 20,000 feet. Without a word between us we closed back in 50 yards or so apart, flying abreast. Finally Shea comes in and says, 'Did you see what I saw?' And I said, 'Yes, I saw what you saw, too.' And as I remember that was about all we said to each other until we got back to England."

Ed Kemmerer, 381st, June 17, 1944: "My last flight was to dive bomb targets near St. Lô. The weather was not as expected, low cloud cover. So we were flying at about 2,000 feet, just under the clouds, when I got hit and a terrific heat came into the cockpit. Not wanting to burn, I bailed out immediately. Fortunately, I had just enough altitude for the chute to open. I landed flat on my back and knocked 'silly'. While getting out of my parachute harness something stung me in my leg the same time I heard the gun shot. They must have yelled at me before the 'warning shot' but with the noise and confusion and my unawareness I didn't hear them. The warning shot nicked my shin, barely drawing blood. I was very happy to be alive. So after sharing my cigarettes and getting a little first aid they took me to their HQs and I started my journey to Stalag Luft III at Sagan, Germany."

The next two articles are extracts from Missing Aircrew Reports for May 30, 1944. They cover the loss of Lts. Dale Rook and Carroll Stearns of the 382nd and both were filed by Marvin Thompson.

382nd Fighter Bomber Squadron (SE)
363rd Fighter Bomber Group (SE)
31 May 1944

STATEMENT

"I last saw Lt. Rook when I made a pass at an ME 410. I heard him call me and say he was on the tail of a FW 190.

I called him and told him to meet me over the smoke from the ME 410 I had shot down. I got no further answer from him and his wingman, Lt. Stearns, came back and joined my flight. Lt. Stearns said he lost Lt. Rook when he broke after the FW 190.

This was 20 miles Northwest of Dessau, Germany, 30 May 1944, at about 1130 hours."

Marvin A. Thompson
1st Lt., Air Corps
382nd Ftr Bomber Sq.

• • •

STATEMENT

"My flight went down to strafe a field at Quackenbruck, Germany, which Lt. Stearns said he saw some planes on.

Lt. Stearns got a hit in his coolant lines as he went across the field. He called and said he was going to bail out. I told him to stay with his ship and reduce his RPMs and manifold pressure. This worked for about 35 minutes when he said it was getting so hot he was going down. He was too low to bail out safely so he bellied in about 20 miles south of the Zuider Zee, in Holland, and was last seen running toward a wooded area."

Marvin A. Thompson
1st Lt., Air Corps
382nd Ftr Bomber Sq.

Almost a loss!
James Brink, 382nd, June 18, 1944:

"The June 18 mission was a dive bombing mission and I got a flak hit that caused a coolant leak that resulted in the engine quitting. I was the only pilot Col. Tipton would allow to fly his airplane and I bailed out of it that day. He was listening on the radio as we approached the field. I was leading "B" Flight and Brownie (John Brown-author) was behind me leading "C" Flight. Brownie called on the radio, 'Brink, you're on fire, Bail out, Bail out, Bail out for Christ sakes!'

About the time I heard his first Bail is when the plane shook violently. In about those 3 or 4 seconds, I had jettisoned the canopy, undid my seat belt, stood up, and jumped over the left side. Col. Tipton asked me afterwards if I would have bailed out if Brownie hadn't shouted at me like he did. I really don't know, but it's probably good that I bailed out; there was no place to make a safe belly landing from such a low altitude and most probably the belly landing would have resulted in fire.

I was quite low when I bailed out and didn't have time to unhook my dinghy. It got caught for a moment and I struggled to get it loose, hit the horizontal stabilizer with my left foot (like hitting it with a sledge hammer) the pain was so great I held it off the ground on landing and bore the entire brunt on my right foot. Made about one swing from leaving the plane, parachute streaming, caught, and I hit the ground. Landed in Lady Bennett's yard, she had been Head of the British Red Cross in WW I. Her houseman carried me to her bedroom, quite swank and luxurious. Dr. Ed Foster, the 382nd Squadron Flight Surgeon, arrived very soon and examined me. I had no visible injury and Lady Bennett insisted that I stay and recuperate. Enid, who I married in July, came to visit me at Lady Bennett's house and had dinner with her. I had to stay in bed because of sore neck muscles, I couldn't lift my head off the pillow without help. I stayed there for a couple of days and Dr. Foster came and said, 'We have to get you out of here, she won't let you go.' So, back to the squadron I went. I started back on combat 22 June."

Latecomer
Wallace King joined the 382nd Fighter Squadron as operations were winding down. He shares some of his experiences during his short time with the 363rd.

"After an uneventful voyage across the North Atlantic, theater orientation at Goxhill, a Glenn Miller concert near Portsmouth, and a C-47 ride to Normandy, myself and several other replacement pilots arrived in the dead of night (did anyone ever arrive at another time) at the 363rd strip on the Cherbourg Peninsula. The date was early August. The group of replacement pilots included Larry Kuhl, Robert Torbet, Kenneth Eaton, and Ken Wackerbarth. All the group except Eaton had come from the cadet class of 44-C, graduating from Eagle Pass, TX. We had trained in P-40's at Tallahassee, FL. Our first experience in a Mustang was at Goxhill, England. So here we were ready to take on the Luftwaffe with about 30 hours transition in war-weary P-51's.

There was little, if any, formal structure to the squadron. I don't remember it flying many missions. My buddies and I filled our time roaming around the area, sticking our noses into concrete bunkers of the Atlantic Wall, rifling through personal effects of German soldiers in abandoned wooden barracks.

If there was any combat training by the existing pilots, I don't remember it. One day Kuhl, Eaton, Torbet, and myself took four P-51s up to practice formation flying. They looked new compared to the mixmatched wing and tail models flown in England. Larry led the flight, Torbet on his wing, I the element leader and Eaton on my wing. Following some close formation flying, Larry signaled us into trail arrangement and he began a loop. About a third of the way through I realized my speed was too slow to complete the top. Shortly, Torbet stalled out in front of me and headed earthward. I sloshed through a half roll, wallowing in a shallow dive to regain control speed. A look over my shoulder revealed Eaton pointing up with no airspeed. Naturally, a whip stall occurred followed by an inverted spin. I watched in horror as the Mustang flashed smaller and smaller toward the French countryside. An explosion was expected at any second. Miraculously the spin stopped and the craft leveled at what appeared to be treetop level from my altitude. I lost sight of Eaton and didn't see him again until landing at the strip. Reviewing the flight, Ken didn't seem distraught as I expected, but he knew it was a close call. I inquired of Larry why he didn't make the loop tighter and faster. He replied he thought we could cut him off, making tighter circles than he, as was the practice in horizontal turns. My reply was that I don't think that principle holds for vertical loops!

One evening my name appeared on the mission board for the next day. Excitement wouldn't be the correct word for my anticipation. However, the next morning the mission was scrubbed. That was the closest I came to flying combat in a P-51. Within a day or two the group was deactivated. Our little band of replacements was given the choice of remaining to fly photo recon missions in camera planes expected to arrive shortly or transfer to other Ninth fighter groups. Naturally, we didn't know that there was only one other P-51 group remaining in the Ninth Air Force, the 354th.

In a day or two our little group got its marching orders, as all of us opted to remain fighter pilots, not picture takers. Only several years ago did I learn that the 363rd did not fly unarmed photo planes after my departure. Had that been told to us at the time, I am sure all of our little group of replacements would have opted to remain instead of transferring out."

Not So Merry England

Wallace Goodhue, 381st crewchief, explains part of the group's welcome to Great Britain.

"Here is a brief explanation of why we had so few photos of the planes and crews, or landing fields. When we left Camp Kilmer, NJ, to go to the dock and load aboard the 'Queen Elizabeth', we were instructed to load all our handguns, hunting knives, and cameras into a large crate, which was clearly marked FRAGILE-CAMERAS. Not a good move. When we arrived at Glascow, Scotland, to disembark we saw from the deck the dock handlers drop that crate, splitting it open. The cameras and guns walked away in all directions...never to be seen again. Some of the guys had really nice cameras and some were later able to get cheaper ones from home."

Relief Tube Troubles

Wallace Goodhue continues with a story of one pilot's experience with the P-51's relief tube.

"Our pilots and groundcrews had a wonderful relationship. We worked together like a team. We tried to have the planes at their top ability knowing that the pilots would have a long flight ahead. We did not want them to take a swim in the Channel. On one occasion we had a pilot who had a slight speech problem. He stuttered when excited. After a long escort mission, deep into Germany, when returning to England they were attacked by a group of Me-109's that came up through the clouds. Since it had been a long flight, it was time for him to use the relief tube. Not good timing. As the bullets began slicing through the plane he had to pay attention to the action about him, and forget about the relief tube. Upon landing safely he tried to relate to the crew what had happened. He got so excited he stuttered and stuttered. The crew all had a good laugh. After de-briefing, he returned to the line and helped the crew wash out and disinfect the inside of the cockpit, a bit embarrassed."

Photo Section

OPPOSITE
Top: 380th Fighter Squadron pilots in front of Evan McCall's P-39 "Fool's Paradise II" (photo taken while the unit was stationed at Oakland). Back Left to right: Vance, Sharrock, Ray, Hersberger, Williams, Barlow, Johnson, unknown, Fontes, McEachron, Hale. Kneeling Left to right: Haynes, McCall, McKinney, DeLong, Nicholas, Tyler, Reddig, Kerns Sitting Left to right: Cashio, Hill, Bruce, Clemovitz, Fryer.

Bottom: 382nd pilots at Hayward, California. Top Left to right: Bingham, Aldrich, Pawlak, Deeds, Collins, Watson. Third Left to right: Lewis, Theil, W. McGee, Kunz, Bullard, Schmidt. Kneeling Left to right: Rook, Clark, Schillereff, Coble, Heberlein, Boatright. Sitting Left to right: Pollard, Brink, Thompson, Cahill, Pederson.

Right: Four 380th pilots while training at Santa Rosa. Left to right: Charles Reddig, Feodor Clemovitz, Morton Kammerlohr, James E. Hill.

Below: Pilots and ground officers of the 380th while based at Santa Rosa.

Above: Some future 363rd pilots while undergoing transition training, September 1943. Back Left to right: Sawchuck, Stewart Sullivan (382nd), Winn, Charles Shea (381st), Westarnark, Bruce Turner (380th). Front Left to right: William Webb, Joe Thoresz, Gerald Scott (all 381st), John Stricker (382nd).

Below: Result of James Brink's September 21, 1943 crash. Note the aircraft number Is 67 whlch should have been a 381st ship. Serial number was 42-9349.

Brink with his 382nd P-39, #99 "Roscoe II".

James Brink on the wing of his first P-51B, C3-P "Roscoe II", on March 13, 1944.

Another shot of Brink.

Charles Reddig (380th).

Feodor Clemovitz (380th).

Bayard Bingham (382nd).

Keith Jacobs (381st).

General Otto Weyland decorating James Dalglish (381st) with 363rd CO John Ulricson on right. The date was April 29, 1944.

Long time 381st CO Dave Culberson (right) with Weyland.

Roy Benson (380th) getting his Air Medal, also April 29.

Gordon McEachron (380th), Fred Munder (381st) and Thomas Tilson (380th) in the same formation.

Ed Ballinger (380th) on the same date.

Long shot of the April 29 award presentation with left to right being: Culberson, Ulricson, Marshall Cloke (380th), Martin DeLong (380th), Jeremiah Boland (381st), James Carter (381st), then McEachron, Munder, and Tilson.

Edwin Vance (380th).

Deputy CO of the 363rd, Ben Irvin.

Charles Smith (381st).

Donald Lewis (382nd).

Left: Donald Boatright (382nd).

Bruce Carr (380th) This photo was taken later in the war when Carr was a member of the 354th Fighter Group.

Dale Rook (382nd) on his "Pied Piper".

Dave Culberson's 381st P-51B B3-A 43-6458 "Huntin' Trouble".

Neill Ullo (380th).

Martin DeLong (380th) with his crew of "Southern Belle".

Charles Shea (381st) with his first P-51B, B3-B 43-6797 "Snark".

George Doerr, 381st Operations Officer.

Doerr's P-51B, B3-W 43-6426 "Pegasus".

Louis Morrison on the wing of his 382nd ship "Toni Girl".

Charles Shiff (382nd) with his P-51 C3-V 43-6713 "Marion".

Shiff with the crew of "Marion". Left to right: John Pacey (assistant crewchief), Joe McDonald (crewchief), Shiff, John Mahoney (armorer).

Clifford Davis (381st) with his crew of "Lady Joan III". Left to right: Wren Dillard (armorer), Davis, Milton Sims (crewchief), and Robert Poole (assistant).

John Robertson (382nd) with his first P-51B "Donna Mae".

William Bullard (382nd) with the crew of his "El Malo Hombre", C3-X 43-6830.

Joe Santarlasci (382nd) standing on his Mustang "Rose O'Day" C3-N 43-6859.

Virgil Johnson (381st) and the crew of "Little Jinnie". Left to right are Johnson, Joe Shull (armorer), and D.L. Jackson (crewchief).

Starboard view of Robert McWherter's 382nd P-51 C3-M 43-6438 "Hoo Flung Dung/City of Paris".

Port view of McWherter's ship.

McWherter's old "Hoo Flung Dung" now coded C3-U.

Unidentified 382nd pilot with P-51C C3-I 42-102992.

Felix Kozaczka (382nd).

The Winged Mustang insignia of the 381st Fighter Squadron.

Right: Marvin Thompson (382nd).

Below: Joe Thoresz (381st) with his crew of B3-Z 42-106740 "Honk Honk".
Left to right: Jess Greer (armorer), Riley Courreges (assistant), James Evans
(crewchief).

Another shot of Thoresz and his ship.

Ralph Tyler (left) and James Hill (380th) with Tyler's A9-T "Honey Belle".

Ray Schillereff (382nd) and the crew of C3-L "Princess Margaret".

Curry Wilson (382nd) with some ground personnel. Left to right: Adrian Zielke (armorer), Joe Signore (engineering clerk), William Trainer (parachute).

James B. Tipton (left) while he was Deputy CO of the 366th Fighter Group. On right is Dyke F. Meyer, 366th Commander.

Walter Whited (381st).

Don Williams (382nd).

Right: Fred Munder (381st).

Merle Kellogg (380th) on the wing of his A9-X 43-6512 "It Sends Me".

Kellogg with his crewchief Howard Mosier.

Ben Williams (381st).

Richard Asbury (382nd).

Below: Asbury with his crew of C3-R "Queenie II". Left to right: unknown, Jack Larson (assistant), George Linkinhoker (crewchief).

Williams with his groundcrew.

Right: Ed Vesely (381st).

Below: Vesely with his P-51B B3-R 43-7138 "Rex". On left is armorer Robert Lewis.

Ed Pawlak (382nd).

Gerald Clough (380th) with the crew of "Corky-Anne". Left to right: Wallace Winkler (crewchief), Clough, Jesse Foster (assistant).

Gordon McEachron (380th) and his "Beachcomber II".

Another shot of McEachron and his P-51B.

James Clark (382nd).

Robert Leety (381st).

Clark and the crew of C3-G "The Mighty Midget". Left to right: Tom Strzynski (armorer), Emanuel Ehlenberger (crewchief), Pete Sikula (assistant).

Ray Wisner (380th & HdQts).

Robert Lamar (382nd).

Lamar with his crew of C3-X 42-106621. Left to right: Morris Easterly (crewchief), Fred Nelson (assistant), Allen Driver (armorer).

John Brown (382nd) with the crew of C3-D 42-106647 "Big Mac Junior".

Robert McGee (382nd) and the crew of C3-A 42-106486 "Virginia" In background is Brown's C3-D.

John Brown (382nd).

Warren Jones (381st).

Jack Warner (382nd).

Lee Webster (382nd).

Patrick Henry (381st).

Richard Johnson (381st).

John Stricker (382nd).

Elmer Odell (382nd).

Bruce Turner (380th).

Another shot of Turner.

Ken Doran (381st).

Ward Miller (381st).

Ed Kemmerer (381st).

381st pilots Left to right: Shea, Thoresz, Williams, Davis Tucker.

381st pilots Left to right: Charles Stuart, Norm Jacobson, Jeremiah Boland, Gerald Scott.

More 381st fliers Back Left to right: Fuller McCowan, Shea, Fred Trumbower, Tucker Center: Harold Baer. Front Left to right: Howard Marks, Gerald Scott, James Newman.

Evan McCall, 380th CO and Operations Officer.

Albert Johnson (380th) in his A9-V 42-106485 "Maggie's Drawers".

Norm Jacobson's 381st P-51B B3-F 43-6505.

Davis Tucker's B3-G 43-6979 "Tarheel Special" of the 381st.

Alex Melancon (380th) and the crew of A9-M.

Another shot of Jim Clark's "The Mighty Midget" of the 382nd.

Ed Pawlak's 382nd P-51C B3-W 43-25045 "My Pal Snookie".

Ed Vesely with his 381st ship B3-R 43-7138 "Rex".

"Lady June" C3-T 43-6447, the 382nd mount of Jack Warner.

Daniel Lowers (381st) and crewchief Wallace Goodhue. Lowers was assigned Charles Shea's old "Snark" when Shea acquired a P-51D.

William Haynes (380th) with his P-51D "Windy City IV".

Charles Lasko (381st) and his P-51D "Buster." Armorer Pete Bedrosian at left.

James Tipton and his personal P-51D "Diablo". Left to right: Ollie Stone (crewchief), Tipton, Carl Swenson (380th Engineering Officer), Dewey Austin (380th Engineering).

Robert McWherter (382nd) and his new P-51D C3-M 44-13380 "Hoo Flung Dung/City of Paris".

James Jabara (382nd).

Joe Santarlasci (382nd).

Two more views of McWherter's P-51D.

Morton Kammerlohr (380th) with his A9-1 44-13706 "Courser II".

Robert Kunz (382nd & HdQts) with his P-51D "El Don".

Right: Gerald Clough (380th) in his "Corky-Anne II".

Robert Heberlein (382nd).

Bedford Underwood (382nd).

Elmer Fogelquist (382nd).

Right: Gerald Scott (381st).

Scott with his crew of B3-M 42-106772 "Lady Patricia".

Left to right: John White (crewchief), Ken Prior (assistant), and Fred Munder (381st) Aircraft is Munder's B3-Y 44-14059 "Skyczar".

John Baird-381st.

Harry Knuppel (381st).

Right: Knuppel with the crew of B3-U 44-13373 "Voodoo" In center is crewchief William Turner, on right is his brother and assistant crewchief Wilton Turner.

Jeremiah Boland (381st).

James Carter (381st).

Boland with his crew of "Frankie Boy", In middle with hat is armorer Don Baird.

Carter and crew with his P-51D "Skywolf" Second from left is James Fitzgerald (armorer).

Charles Gallagher (381st) in his B3-S 44-13340 "Squirrel".

Gallagher with his crew. Left to right are Gallagher, Capt. Robert Foster (Chaplain), John Rousell (armorer), Delton Kuntz (assistant), and on wing Stephen DeMarco (crewchief).

Fred Trumbower (381st).

Trumbower and the crew of "Killer" Far left is armorer Harold Hass.

Two views of Burl Williams (380th) and his "Oklahoma Kid III".

Hugo Pressnall (381st) with his first P-51 "Tear Azz". On left is John Kelly (armorer) with crewchief Eugene Renneker on right.

Norm Jacobson (381st) and the crew of his "Sugarfoot III". Left to right are Dominic Morazzo (crewchief), William Decho (assistant), Bernard Quinn (armorer).

Another shot of Pressnall.

Ralph Yothers (382nd).

Below: Pressnall with the crew of his P-51D B3-1 44-13672 "The Sword of the Spirit". Left to right: Nick Marinelli (assistant), Mike Fekete (crewchief), Carroll Andrinks (armorer).

Charles Shea (381st) with his assistant crewchief Elton Ritchey.

Shea with the crew of his B3-D 44-13396 "One Long Hop". Left to right: Elton Ritchey (assistant), Charles Moyle (armorer), Harold Hansen (crew-chief).

Another view of Shea and Ritchey.

George Decker (381st Engineering Officer), Fred Munder and Shea in front of "One Long Hop".

Gordon McEachron in his new P-51D "Beachcomber III".

David King (382nd).

Norman Ott (382nd).

Below: Pilots of the 382nd gathered around Brown's "Big Mac Junior". Left to right on wings/fuselage: Heberlein, Clark, Brown, Schillereff, Webster. Left to right sitting on wings: McWherter, Jabara. Left to right standing: Brink, Pavelich, Kozaczka, Robertson, Reeves. Behind wing: Santarlasci.

Paul Sparer (381st).

Robert MacDonald (380th & 381st).

Marvin Abramovitz (382nd).

Donald Frye (382nd).

Left: Warren Littlefield (382nd).

Top Brass of the 363rd in late July 1944. Left to right: Morrison (380th CO), Lasko (381st CO), McWherter (382nd CO), Tipton (Group CO).

Donald Ray (380th) and his crew of "Little Chico".

David Wolf, 381st Intelligence Officer.

Unidentified 382nd member (name appears to be F.T. Evans which does not show up on any lists) with Stricker's "Green Hornet".

Below: Charles Shiff's C3-V 43-6713 "Marion" in August 1944. Note it appears to retain the white cowl band and spinner rather than the 382nd's assigned color of yellow.

Bottom: Gerald Scott's B3-M 42-106772 "Patricia Baby" undergoing repairs.

Evan McCall's last 380th Mustang A9-A 44-13309 "Fool's Paradise IV".

James Brink's final 382nd P-51 C3-P 44-13554 "Roscoe II".

"Schuberts' Serenade" of William Schubert (380th).

C3-A 43-6382 of the 382nd.

George Recagno of the 381st. Photo taken while he was on his second tour with the 354th Fighter Group.

381st officers on a German gun emplacement in Cherbourg. Left to right are James Legaskis (Exec), Dave Culberson (CO), James McManus (armament), and Harry Knuppel (Flight Leader).

Norm Jacobson on his B3-V 44-13644 "Sugarfoot III".

Two views of Thomas Killingsworth's 380th P-51B A9-L 43-6706.

Right: Starboard view of Munder's 381st P-51D "Skyczar".

Below: Full starboard shot of Munder's ship.

Bottom: B3-J "Mar Jean III" of the 381st after a forced-landing (It is very possible this was taken after the group had converted to a Tac Recon outfit).

Right: Merle Kellogg's last 380th ship, A9-N 44-14022 "Miss Fire".

Below: 380th P-51D A9-O 44-13841 "Torque Jockey".

Bottom: Another 380th P-51D, this time A9-B 44-13989 "Pat-Mary Pat."

Robert Bowe, 380th armorer, with A9-U Note unusual placement of the code letters with A9 being aft of the national insignia.

Morton Kammerlohr, 380th Operations Officer, with members of the squadron Operations staff. Left to right: Kammerlohr, Joe Sciacca, Richard B. Engleman, Weldon Snively.

Armorer Don Van Sluyters (left) with crewchief Howard Mosier (380th) shown with Kellogg's A9-X "It Sends Me".

380th Engineering personnel. Left to right on wing: John Salay, Anthony Haley, Robert Majnik, David Holbrook, Jess Foster, Charles Cornell. In front is Howard Mosier.

380th mechanics with Richard Miller (assistant) on left and Alvin Wolff (crewchief) on right.

380th Crewchiefs and Assistants of "B" Flight. Back row Left to right: Leo Dreiger, Sol Mallin, Ed Weidlich, Mike Salvage, Wayman Caldwell, Robert Majnik, Leon Prince. Front Left to right: Stan Lench, Jack Kellar, Albert McElroy, Leonard Hackley, Ed Egan.

380th Crewchiefs and Assistants of "C" Flight. Back Left to right: Richard Miller, Lowell Williams, Henry Neinner, John Braubach, Robert Watson, Eugene Black. Front Left to right: Cecil Baker, William Ahern, John McCabe, Howard Mosier, Alvin Wolff.

380th Crewchiefs and Assistants of "D" Flight: Back Left to right: Anthony Haley, Lloyd Miller, Harold Burks, Tom Hanley, Edmund Borkowski, Charles Cornell, Erwin Derrick. Front Left to right: Dave Holbrook, Wilfred Hicks, Charlton Motley, Burl Mitchell, William Blount.

380th Engineering crews in July 1944. Back Left to right: Richard Art, Howard Stevens, Clarence Colyer, Pearl Williams, James Auringer, Herman Blaimier, Cecil Kelly. Front Left to right: Don Judge, Seth Hickerson, Myron Hineman, Chester Podolak, John Grady, Henry Simokat, Toy Toi.

Engineering Section of the 380th in July 1944. Far left standing is Robert Mayer, Assistant Engineering Officer and far right standing is Carl Swenson, Engineering Officer.

Cecil Baker (left) and Eugene Pelizzari, 380th crewchiefs.

380th Engineering personnel. Back Left to right: Ed Weidlich, Howard Mosier, Alvin Wolff, Cecil Baker. Front Left to right: Eugene Pelizzari, "Homer" the dog, Harry Rice, Robert Majnik.

380th armorers in July 1944. #1 Peter Bender, #2 James Christensen, #3 Ivan Wick, #4 Russell Jayne, #5 Mike Seiber, #6 Luther Lewis, #7 Stan Boron.

Trio of 380th crewchiefs. Left to right: Ed Weidlich, John McCabe, Alvin Wolff.

380th armorers James Christensen (left) and Ivan Wick.

Robert Watson (assistant on left) and Alvin Wolff (crewchief) in a photo taken late in the war with a Mustang of the 160th Tac Recon Squadron (formerly the 380th Fighter Squadron).

380th crewchief Wallace Winkler in one of his P-51's.

381st Crewchiefs and Assistants of "A" Flight.

381st Crewchiefs and Assistants of "B" Flight.

381st Crewchiefs and Assistants of "C" Flight.

381st Crewchiefs and Assistants of "D" Flight.

P-51 of the 381st undergoing maintenance.

381st armorer Bernie Quinn working on a P-51.

Armament section of the 381st (Photo taken after becoming a Tac Recon unit but all the men in the photo except Maj. Rose served with the 381st). Left to right First row: Maj. James Rose, Pete Bedrosian, Miguel Calderone, Ed Walczak, James Fitzgerald, Charles Moyle, Haynes Williams, Lt. Jerome Ziger Second row: Leo Manning, Orlean Boen, Nicholas Litterio, Don Baird, Harold Hass. Third row: Van Hawkins, Arthur Kelsey, Norm Lee, Alex Slutsky, Irving Jones Fourth row: Robert Heyne, Joe Shull, Herbert Haase, Clint Smith, Richard Heath. Top upper left: Bernard Quinn, Wren Dillard.

Julian LeBlanc, Adjutant for both the 381st and 382nd.

Above: 382nd Engineering members of "A" Flight.

Below: 382nd Engineering members of "B" Flight.

382nd Engineering members of "C" Flight.

382nd Engineering members of "D" Flight Standing far left is George Linkinhoker.

Trio of 382nd fuel crew personnel (photo taken after becoming a Tac Recon unit) Left to right: Farris Mansfield, Robert MacGown, George Henning.

Right: George Henning, 382nd fuel crew.

Below: 382nd refueling crew; On wheel is Farris Mansfield, with arm on fender is George Henning, and far right is Robert MacGown.

Above: 382nd Armament Section with C3-Z in background.   Below: Flight and Line Chiefs of the 382nd with unknown officer on far right.

Radio mechanics, metalsmiths, and carpenters of the 382nd.

382nd Operations personnel. Officer third from right is unknown (possibly Brown?).

382nd Transportation Department. Far right kneeling is John Maciolek and center kneeling is Charles Snyder.

Headquarters Section of the 382nd. Kneeling on far right is Richard Buckle, Adjutant.

Mess Section of the 382nd.

363rd Fighter Group Aircraft in Profile

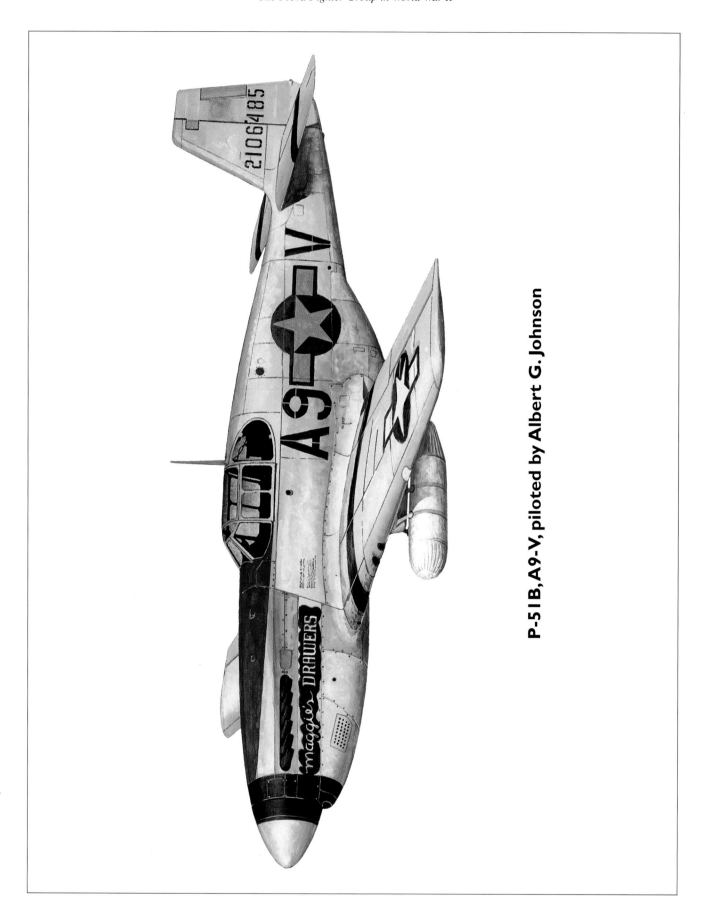

P-51B, A9-V, piloted by Albert G. Johnson

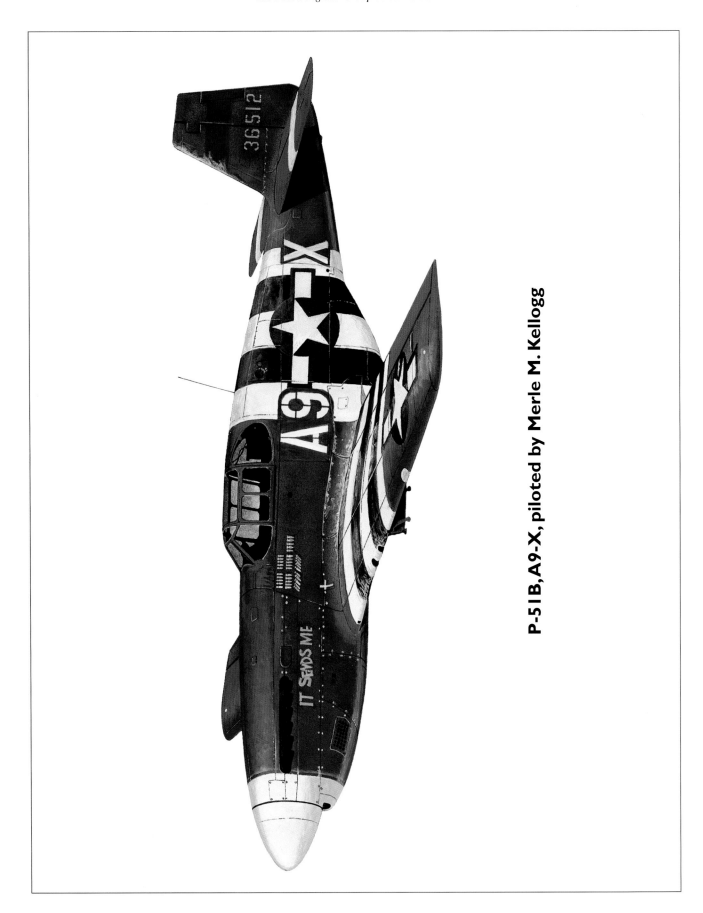

P-51B, A9-X, piloted by Merle M. Kellogg

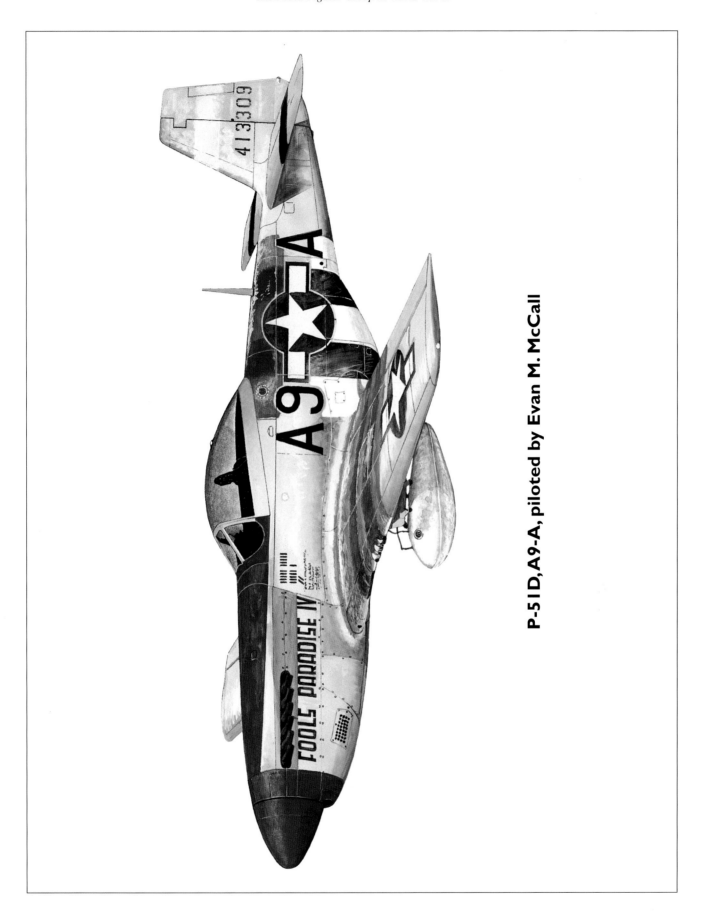

P-51D, A9-A, piloted by Evan M. McCall

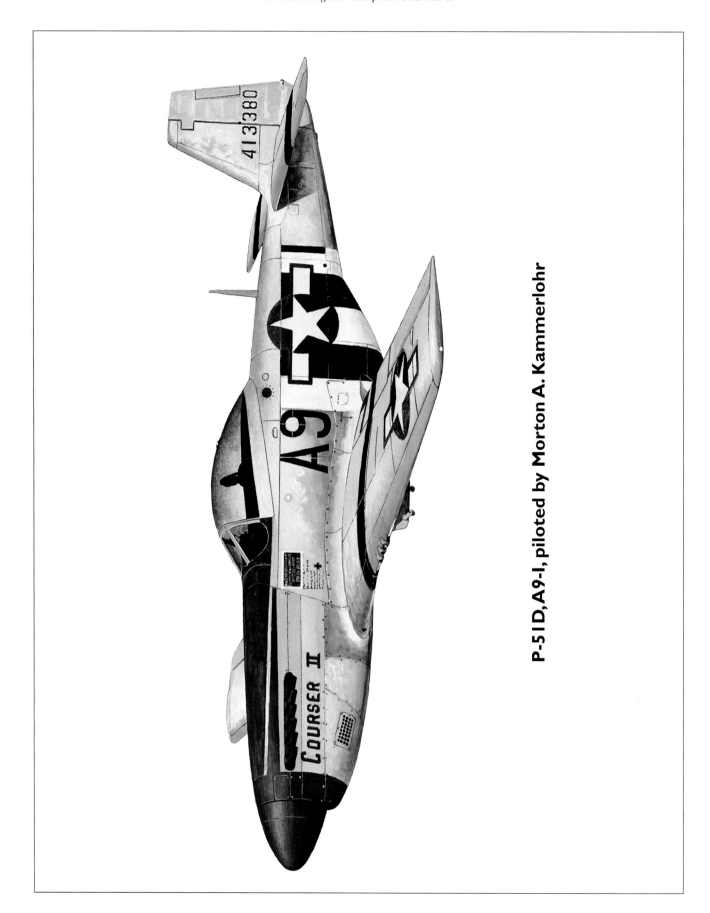

P-51D, A9-I, piloted by Morton A. Kammerlohr

P-51B, B3-B, piloted by Charles E. Shea

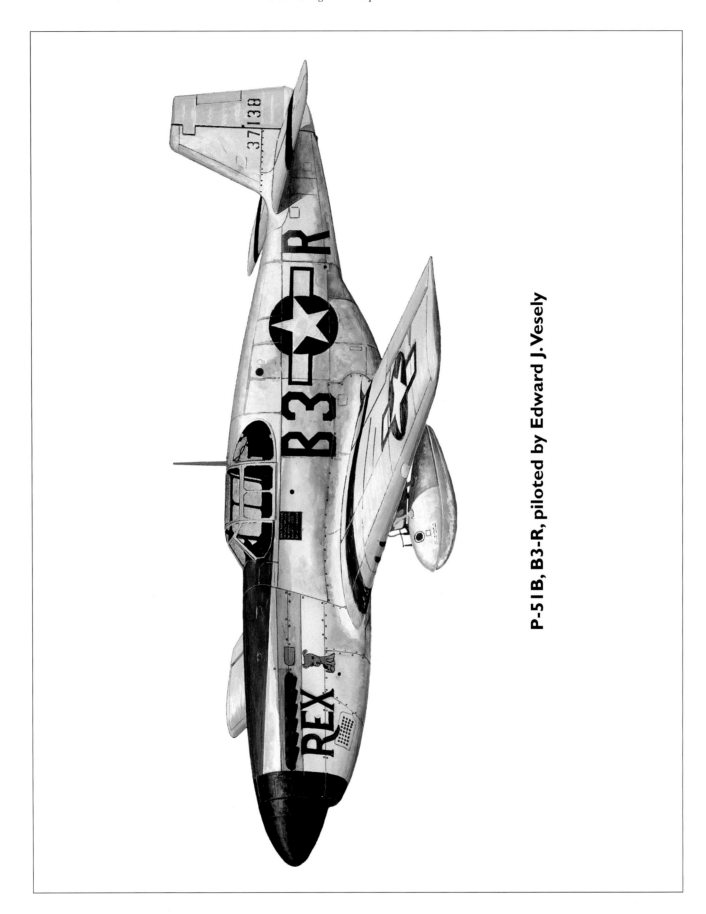

P-51B, B3-R, piloted by Edward J. Vesely

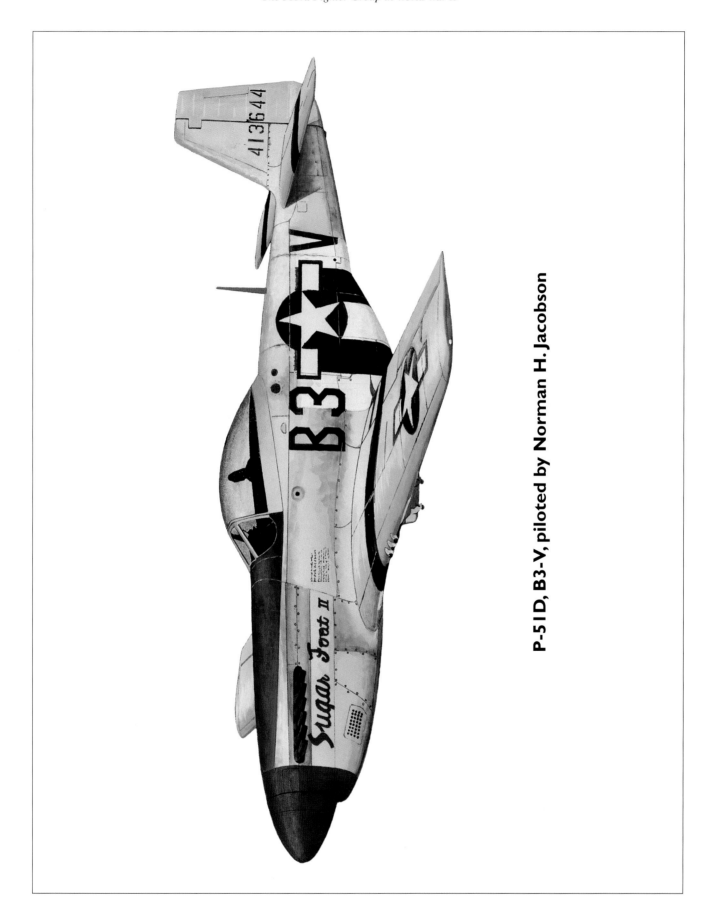

P-51D, B3-V, piloted by Norman H. Jacobson

P-51D, B3-U, piloted by Harry D. Knuppel

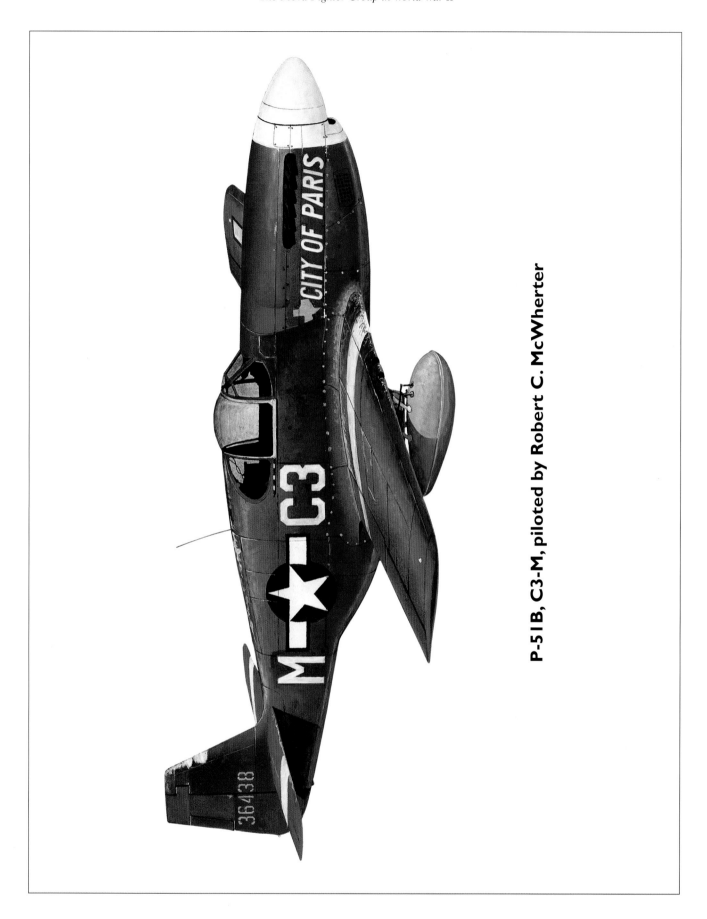

P-51B, C3-M, piloted by Robert C. McWherter

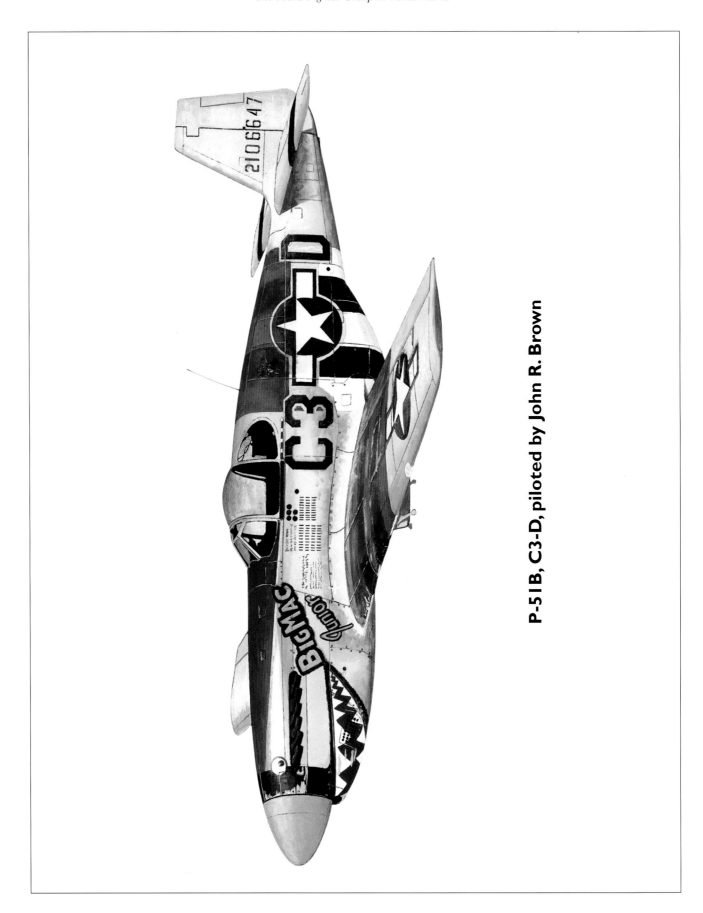

P-51B, C3-D, piloted by John R. Brown

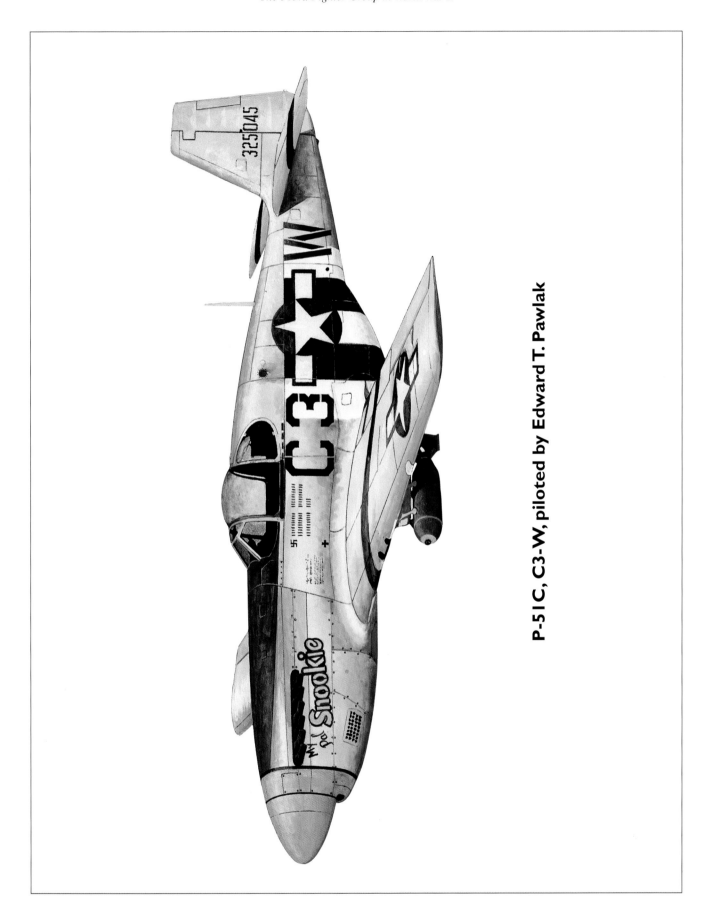

P-51C, C3-W, piloted by Edward T. Pawlak

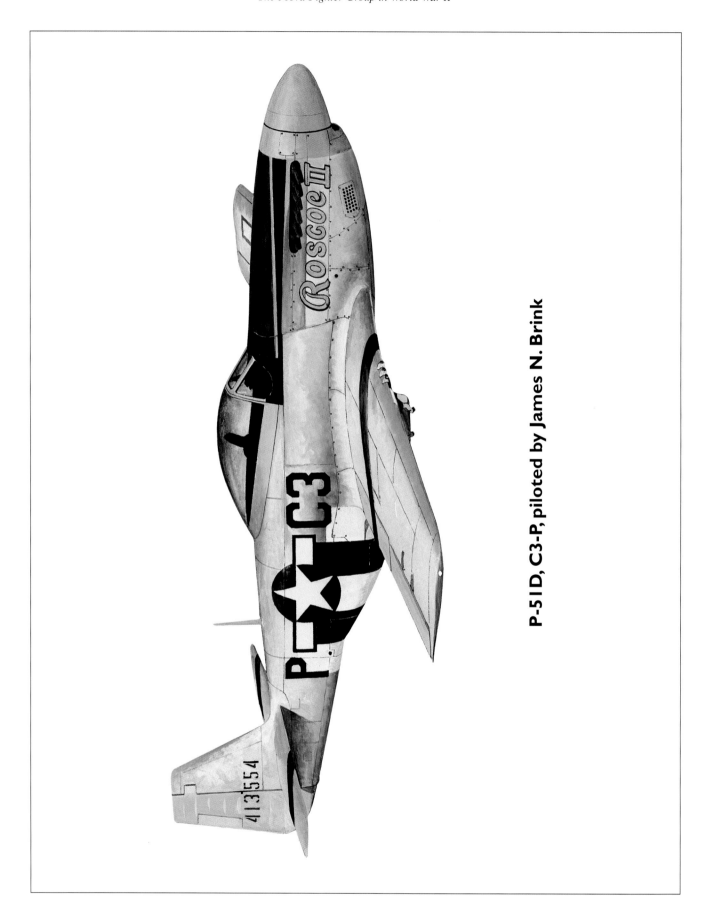

P-51D, C3-P, piloted by James N. Brink

Name Index